Incest

The Story of Three Women

Dianne Cleveland
Director
Peachtree City Counseling Center

Lexington Books
D.C. Heath and Company/Lexington, Massachusetts/Toronto

Library of Congress Cataloging-in-Publication Data

Cleveland, Dianne, 1945–
  Incest : the story of three women.

  Bibliography: p.
  Includes index.
  1. Incest victims—United States—Case studies.
2. Adult child abuse victims—United States—Case
studies. 3. Incest—United States. I. Title.
HQ72.U53C54   1986   306.7'777   85-45435
ISBN 0-669-11729-3 (alk. paper)
ISBN 0-669-12726-4 (pbk.: alk. paper)

Published simultaneously in Canada
Printed in the United States of America
Casebound International Standard Book Number: 0-669-11729-3
Paperbound International Standard Book Number: 0-669-12726-4
Library of Congress Catalog Card Number: 85-45435

The paper used in this publication meets the minimum requirements of
American National Standard for Information Sciences—Permanence of
Paper for Printed Library Materials, ANSI Z39.48–1984.

The last numbers on the right below indicate the number and date of printing.

10 9 8 7 6 5 4 3 2

95 94 93 92 91 90 89 88 87 86

For my parents
and
to the memory of my grandmother, Bert

Contents

Tables

Foreword

This is a book alive with relevant and timely information concerning the problem of incest. Dr. Cleveland has taken what may turn out to be the social and therapeutic topic of this decade and allowed the issues to speak through the lives of those who have lived them.

Child sexual abuse within the family almost always leaves its mark on the child in later life. This is the point at which Dr. Cleveland became involved in the topic and developed an interest in researching the development of the lives of its victims. Her experience as coleader of a therapy group for women who were former victims provided not only the interest, but also the sensitivity, to conduct such a study. She chose a qualitative method in order to study in depth a few subjects, each of whom reveals her own personal life response to a childhood sexual relationship in the family.

This book answers the need of many professionals for a readable, informative work on incest. Its gripping content is matched only by its presentation, and it should be equally informative to the general public.

Donald A. Randall, Jr.
Executive Director
Family Counseling Service
of Athens, Georgia

Acknowledgments

I t is a difficult task to express adequately on paper the gratitude I feel toward the many people who have helped to make my dream of this book a reality.

The book grew out of the research I conducted in order to complete the requirements of the doctoral program in Counseling and Human Development at the University of Georgia. First and foremost I would like to thank my major professor, advisor, and friend, Dr. Jack M. Sink. Without Jack's willingness to be flexible and to allow me to write the first qualitative dissertation in our department, this book would not have been written. Thanks also go to the other members of my doctoral committee who were willing to learn along with me—Dr. Warren Bonney, Dr. Sam Mitchell, Dr. Robert Pollack, Dr. Karen Wampler—and to Dr. Judith Goetz, who introduced me to qualitative research. Their support, encouragement, and enthusiasm for this project have been invaluable.

My interest in the long-term consequences of sexual abuse began four years ago when Don Randall and I embarked on the adventure of coleading a weekly therapy group for adult females who had experienced an incestuous relationship in childhood. Over the years I have never ceased to be amazed at the strength of these women who come and share their most intimate thoughts, feelings, and experiences. I have seen amazing changes in these women once they reveal their incest "secret," and it is heard and accepted in a loving, supportive atmosphere. It appears to be healing just to learn that they are not alone in their experience.

I have come to believe that incest has no simple solution. This book is for all the women who have been willing to share with me the pain and the triumphs in their lives. They were the impetus for this book.

The process of conducting research and writing a book is stressful at best. My experience was made easier by my friends Fred Breme, Lynn Chastain, Linda Franz, Barbara Gervais, Margaret Mittiga, Judy Mote, Sancy Robey, Jo Sink, and Betty Tanner, who were always available to listen, and each, in his or her own way, to remind me to take the time to laugh. Also thanks to my roommate, Wanda Faurie, who lived with my dissertation on our dining room table for six months!

Dr. Nancy Vrecheck has been a constant support to me during our doctoral programs. My journey to a Ph.D. has been made much easier because it was shared with a friend.

Also, thanks to my good friend Max Cleland, who, at the times when I did not think I could write or rewrite another word, was always there in his unique fashion to remind me, "Don't worry, Hemingway rewrote the ending of *A Farewell to Arms* twenty-eight times!"

Finally, the three women whose lives make up this book deserve a special thanks. They each generously opened their lives and shared their most intimate thoughts and feelings concerning their incestuous experiences. I hope this book will offer some insight for professionals who will be working with clients who have been sexually abused. Perhaps more important, I hope this book will offer comfort to adolescents who are currently in an incestuous relationship and to adults who are struggling with an incestuous past. I hope that each will benefit from our efforts. But, most of all, I hope that we have shown that lives can be changed, and that by sharing the incest "secret" we rob it of its power.

1
Introduction

I ncest is an emotionally charged topic carrying strong cultural taboos. When incest is discovered, it defies our basic values. The feelings evoked range from disbelief and revulsion to fascination and outrage. While there have been an increasing number of books written on incest, there still exist widespread misconceptions.

Incest has existed throughout the ages. It is a taboo that is found in all known cultures—ancient, primitive, and civilized. However, there have been notable exceptions throughout history. For example, ancient Egyptian pharoahs were permitted to marry a sibling of the same father, but prohibited from marrying a sibling of the same mother. Incest has also been tolerated in some European royal families as well as permitted in some primitive tribes during religious ceremonies. Although the nature and strength of the taboo vary from culture to culture, incest rules remain the most sternly enforced regulations for sexual contact and marriage relationships throughout the world. Originally the taboo was enforced by the tribe and later by the church. Today, it is enforced by the courts as well. It is a legal mandate in all fifty states to report cases of incest.

The universal taboo has been explained as deriving from an innate biological mandate against inbreeding. It developed into a social measure whose purpose is to maintain the integrity of the family unit in order to avoid role confusion among family members and to eliminate disruptive and competitive behaviors. However, as states have passed more effective legislation mandating the reporting of incest, the magnitude of the incest problem is slowly emerging. It now appears that we, as a society, have been ignorant of the facts about incest. Keeping incest a taboo and a forbidden subject has not prevented sex in the family; it has simply prevented recognition of the problem. Authorities agree that the number of cases reported and confirmed are only a fraction of those that go unreported.

The entire subject of sexuality is surrounded by more positive and negative emotions and more conflict than any other human activity. If this is true for the general population, and we know that the consequences of sexual abuse for children are more psychological than physical, then from a long-range mental health perspective there is a need to be concerned.

The current attitudes and laws regarding incest are myth-ridden and ineffective (Giaretto, 1982). States differ greatly in their legal definitions of child sexual abuse, specifically incest, and the penalties for the offenders. There is a need for professionals and lay persons alike to become aware of the predisposing conditions in incestuous families and the potential emotional consequences for those involved. In this way appropriate interventions might be developed and implemented immediately once sexual abuse is discovered.

While incest remains a taboo, discussion of the problem no longer is. Incest is believed to be far more common than anyone has been able to document (Justice and Justice, 1979). Incest may even be increasing as a result of the great changes that are taking place in family life today.

Part of the reason for the lack of emphasis on and disbelief of childhood incestuous experiences probably dates back to the works of Sigmund Freud. Freud thought that incestuous wishes were universal among human children (Lester, 1975). He concluded that incestuous fantasies rather than overt incestuous acts were critically important in personality development and at the root of neuroses (Freud, 1938). Psychoanalysts therefore subsequently used these fantasies of incest as a major construct in their theory of personality. The firm establishment of the fantasy mode led Freud and other psychoanalysts to discount their patients' reports of sexual abuse during childhood. Unfortunately, this perspective has continued, resulting in significant skepticism on the part of professionals in accepting the validity of incestuous relations reported by patients.

The feminist movement has been instrumental in focusing attention on the circumstances and consequences of childhood incest and sexual abuse (Herman, 1981). Sexual abuse has emerged as the major form of child abuse in the United States today (Finkelhor, 1979). Although sexual abuse has become the fastest growing form of abuse reported to public agencies, it has been surmised that 90 percent of the cases go unreported (Blumberg, 1978). Reasons for the low rate of disclosure include: the social taboo, the fear of the community's reaction and the stigmatization of the family, the possible disruption of the family, the reality of possible criminal punishment, the lack of available treatment programs and professional help, and the guilt feelings of those involved.

Vital statistics on incest in our society are also difficult to obtain because of the differing definitions of sexual abuse in state laws. In addition, there is a bias in reporting that tends to favor reporting cases of families of lower socioeconomic classes and covering up cases of families in higher social classes. However, we do know that incest crosses all racial, religious, educational, and socioeconomic lines. It also crosses all traditional psychiatric classifications. Our current knowledge about perpetrators of incest contradicts the old stereotypes that the offender was mentally ill, sexually perverted, alcoholic, psychopathic, retarded, uneducated, unskilled, and/or a drug addict. Incest is a complicated subject with no simple solution. It is important to remember that the whole environment of the family is involved in contributing to the conditions in which incest occurs.

The studies that do exist show that as many as 15 to 30 percent of all American women and 5 to 10 percent of all American men were sexually abused as children by an adult (Finkelhor, 1979). Estimates further suggest that as many as 50,000 children are abused sexually by parents or guardians each year (Masters, Johnson & Kolodny, 1982). In a study conducted by DeFrancis, a parent or a surrogate was involved in 72 percent of the cases either by perpetration or by acts of omission (Masters, Johnson & Kolodny, 1982).

Although boys are not immune, the majority of victims are girls. Father–son, mother–daughter, and mother–son incestuous relationships are thought to be uncommon and, because of the scarcity of such cases, the impact of such relationships is not known.

Research data going back to the pioneering work of Kinsey in 1948 indicates that brother–sister incest is about five times as common as father–daughter incest (Kinsey, Pomeroy, Martin & Gebhard, 1953). However, such relationships are thought to be transient and may be relatively free from the damaging psychological repercussions that often result from a father–daughter incestuous relationship (Meiselman, 1981).

Since incest tends to remain a "family secret," it is still difficult to make generalizations about its etiology, effects, and treatment outcomes. The response to the incest differs significantly depending on the frequency, duration, intensity, and nature of the sexual acts; the child's relationship to the perpetrator; and the family's and the community's support of the child when the incest is reported.

Most of the studies of incest appear to involve cases that have been identified in the following ways: (1) self-reported, with incest as the presenting problem; (2) the perpetrator is in jail, usually for other offenses, and subsequently is identified as having been involved in incest; (3) the daughter develops behavioral problems, and professional help is sought; and (4) the daughter becomes pregnant as a result of the incestuous relationship.

Boekelheide (1978) hypothesized that less than 25 percent of the young female victims escape psychological trauma from the incestuous experience. Many adult females seeking psychotherapy for sexual dysfunction, sexual maladjustment, marital problems, problems with relationships in general, and prostitution or suicide attempts have histories of sexual molestation as children.

Statement of the Problem

The prevailing opinion in the literature, although not uncontested (DeMott, 1980), is that an incestuous relationship in the home poses many threats to the normal development and adjustment of the child. But, at present, these speculated "influences" remain just that—opinions untested.

Clearly, it seems important to begin the investigation of the long-term effects of incestuous experiences on children because of (1) the wide variety of clinical patients who have incestuous histories, and (2) the theoretical contributions to the psychology of parent–child relations.

Purpose of the Study

The purposes of this research are: (1) to identify specific consequences to the victim as an adult of a childhood sexual experience with the father; (2) to compare adjustment and personality characteristics of three women who have experienced such a relationship; (3) to produce inferences and implications for the counseling profession that will promote effective counseling with clients who have had such experiences; and (4) to stimulate additional inquiry into the area of consequences to an adult of a childhood sexual relationship with the father.

Significance of the Study

Previous research has viewed the long-term effects of an incestuous experience in a fragmented manner. What we do not know is how these experiences fit into a developmental life span. One primary concern of this book is to create a developmental perspective, and also to generate a broader view and deeper understanding of the dynamics and consequences involved in father–daughter incest.

2
An Overview of Incest

S peculations about incestuous experiences are numerous. Some sociol-
ogists believe incest occurs as a result of a long-standing family disorganization. Both parents have usually suffered from severe early
deprivation themselves, and this has compromised their ability to parent
maturely (Rosenfeld, 1977; Wells, 1981). Because of this lack of ability to
parent, the boundaries between the generations that support distinct social
and psychological roles for parent and child have been obliterated (Yates,
1982).

Incestuous families have been analyzed most commonly in terms of the
concept of role reversal between the mother and daughter. The disruption in
roles is seen to result not only in strained interpersonal relationships, but
more importantly in an altered family structure (Forward & Buck, 1978;
Kempe & Kempe, 1984; Sgroi, 1982). These alterations in family structure
from the incestuous relationship are thought to have a wide variety of effects
on the family, most of them detrimental.

The responsibility of the child is thus changed both qualitatively and
quantitatively insofar as she has to take on burdens, tasks, responsibilities,
and roles in addition to those she would normally assume. This limits the
flexibility these girls have in playing other roles that would be appropriate for
them. For example, the focus on sexual learning in childhood detracts from
appropriate social learning with peers.

Another major effect is that the child who experiences incest lacks appropriate parental role models with whom to identify. Incestuous families tend
to be patriarchal with the father demanding complete submission from family
members (DeYoung, 1982). The father therefore is less able to model appropriate masculine behaviors in place of aggression, dominance, and physically
abusive behavior.

The mother in these families tends to be weak, unassertive, dependent,
and passive (Peters, 1976). She generally is unable or unwilling to protect her
children. She may even contribute to the child's ongoing victimization by
failing to transmit effective coping and self-protecting skills.

Discipline and power relations between parent and child are speculated to be a problem in a home with incest occurring. Difficulty in disciplining and maintaining control of the child can greatly affect the child's evaluation of the parents. Relationships with siblings are also adversely affected if the siblings become aware of the incestuous relationship (Giaretto, 1982). Siblings either become isolated from one another because of the secrecy involved in the incest, or there is tension, jealousy, or anger about the possible favored treatment or attention one is receiving from the father.

Parents who are less able to manage the physical care of their children may not be able to complete the normal bonding process between parent and child that is essential for healthy development. The inability of the father to differentiate an affectionate touch from an invitation for sexual activity can result in a destructive concept and fear of sexuality (Summit & Kryso, 1978). The child may come to feel that she has no worth except as a sexual object. She often never learns the role of daughter adequately and is confused about the distinction between sex and affection.

Being a good parent involves not only the practical care of the child, but also the giving of emotional security and love. The victim of incest may feel a sense of betrayal from both of her parents if her complying with her father's wishes is an attempt to fulfill needs that are normally met in other ways. The cooperation of the child can be obtained through the adult's position of dominance, a bribe of material goods or money, a threat of physical violence (not sexual), or a misrepresentation of the moral standards and of the implications of an incestuous relationship. For example, the child may cooperate out of a need for love, affection, attention, or a sense of loyalty to the adult. Once she realizes that society frowns on incestuous relationships, she may feel used, abused, and betrayed by her father.

Another level of influence on children hypothesized to result from incest with a parent is the social stigma attached once a disclosure is made. The child learns to see herself and her family as different. The child often feels shame and tries to conceal the incestuous relationship out of fear of possible ostracism. Often the reactions of adults and the larger community are more disturbing than the incestuous experience itself.

The psychology of parent–child relations provides a larger context within which this research can be set. Theory and research on the relations between parental characteristics and the child's adjustment point to aspects of parenting conducive to normal development of the child. They also point to personality and behavioral variables in children that are important in assessing and understanding the impact of an incestuous experience on children.

A conceptual as well as methodological difficulty in research on incestuous relationships is inherent—the distinction between association and causation (Walters & Stinnet, 1971). This is an important distinction in the present study, since variables other than the father–daughter sexual relationship may differ in the home environment of children who experience such a relationship. Thus, while different patterns of adjustment and personality characteristics may be associated with the incest, it cannot be assumed that the incestuous relationship has caused the difference.

Parental Attitudes and Behavior

Research points to parental warmth as a crucial factor affecting a child's development. Parental warmth is positively correlated with variables associated with emotional, social, and intellectual development. Children with warm, loving parents are more mature, intellectually achieving, emotionally stable, psychologically adjusted, and able to form intimate relationships than are children of rejecting parents.

Since parental behavior has a pervasive influence on the child's adjustment, the present study will assess the behavior of the parents toward their children as perceived by the child. Schaefer (1965) concluded after reviewing a large number of studies that children's reports of parental behavior are valid.

Parental Identification

It has been hypothesized that children acquire personality characteristics through the process of identification. However, the conceptualization and mechanism of identification is by no means consistent or clear. There is evidence, however, that (1) parent–child similarities in behavior, personality, and attitudes occur; and (2) parental variables such as nurturance, warmth, dominance, control, involvement with the family, and child-rearing practices affect identification with the parent (Bandura, 1969).

Parental Influence

Traditionally, most research has focused on the mother–child relationship. However, a growing body of literature points to the importance of the father's influence on human development (Biller, 1971; Lamb, 1975). It has become increasingly clear that the father not only plays a role in sex-role development, but also has an impact on cognitive, emotional, and behavioral functioning. Hamilton (1977) found that the behavioral patterns of fathers positively related to competence, motivation, self-esteem, successfulness, and creativity in children.

In contrast, personality maladjustment and behavioral disorders in children are associated with fathers who provide inadequate fathering. Professionals generally agree that most children are handicapped if they have experienced paternal inadequacy or deprivation.

In summary, incest violates a tenaciously maintained taboo in most societies. While it is acknowledged by professionals that incest is a complicated subject, there does appear to be a consensus that a childhood sexual experience with one's parent may have profound effects on later development (Burgess, Groth, Holmstrom & Sgroi, 1978).

It must be remembered that sexual abuse of children crosses all ethnic, educational, and socioeconomic boundaries. However, sexual child abuse, specifically incest, does not occur in what is typically described as a "healthy" family, and therefore there are other serious difficulties for the developing child (Kempe & Kempe, 1978). Poor intelligence combined with poor judgment, poor impulse control, lack of knowledge about children, lack of emphasis on child development, large family size with little attention paid to the individual child, and poor parental role models may all contribute to the failure of the parents in meeting the child's needs for nurturance and protection until the child is mature enough to seek out his or her own relationships.

3
Methodology

I n this chapter, I would like to describe briefly the research design and the justification for its choice. I also will describe the selection procedures used for obtaining the subjects, the setting and time involved in the field, my experiences, and the roles I assumed in each case. Finally, I will present the techniques adopted to analyze the information obtained and what I perceive as limitations of this study.

Research Design

The method of research for this study was the life-history approach (Denzin, 1970; White, R.W., 1963) and was influenced by the writing of Levinson (1978) and R.W. White (1974). I believed this was the most appropriate method for the investigation of the patterns of development in the lives of three women who had experienced, as young children, sexual relationships with their natural fathers. Until now, very little research has been conducted on the long-term consequences of such a relationship. The works of Forward and Buck (1978), Meiselman (1981), Kempe and Kempe (1984), Justice and Justice (1979), and Herman (1981) are beginning efforts to utilize elements of qualitative research methods for investigating the long-term effects of such sexual experiences during childhood. Thus, I decided that because of the depth, fullness, and detail of life-history narratives, the data would be useful for both heightening the awareness of counselors and the stimulation of additional research.

One goal of the life history is a holistic portrayal of a person. This approach provides a complete picture of a particular person, a unique entity with his or her own personal meaning and constellation of relationships emerging from the context within which he or she exists (Patton, 1980). Even if we examine small parts or brief segments of human affairs, they must still be understood as parts of a system, and as brief segments of a life-long process (White, R.W., 1963).

This paradigm seeks to capture what people have to say in their own words. It provides depth and detail in order to find what people's lives, experiences, and interactions mean to them in their own terms. The research consists of detailed descriptions of situations, people, interactions, observed behavior, direct quotations, nonverbal behavior, and the verbal interactions between the subject and myself.

This type of research (phenomenological qualitative) emphasizes the subjective aspects of people's behavior. Such researchers attempt to understand individuals from their own point of view (Bogdan & Biklen, 1982; Rogers, 1980). The researcher's insight becomes the key instrument for analysis. It is up to the researcher to present sufficient data that his readers have an adequate basis for analyzing the findings themselves. Since the ability to generalize and replicate the findings is not the focus of a descriptive study such as this, the reliability and validity of the study depend on how fully the phenomena and setting are described (LeCompte & Goetz, 1982).

This method is still evolving, and finding the questions becomes one of the products of data collection. The questions posed may be modified, or discarded if found inappropriate. In this way, the study actually structures the research rather than searches for data or evidence to prove or disprove hypotheses formulated before the study began. It is as if one were putting together a picture that takes shape as the parts are collected and examined.

I designed a lengthy interview instrument in order to provide as much structure as possible and also to cut down on the possibility of interviewer bias. Open-ended questions were used in order to promote flexibility and to gain depth in the responses. Thus, the interviews had the advantage of being adaptable to each subject. The assumption underlying life-history interviews is that the individual's perspective is meaningful, knowable, and able to be made explicit. It is assumed that the subject has a pronounced sense of individuality and a view of his or her past life as one that is distinguishable from other lives.

Selection of the Participants

There is no attempt to claim that the three women in this study are representative of some larger population. This study has not "sampled," but rather has investigated the experiences of these three women. Yet, the characters and experiences of these women are very similar to large segments of the population of incest victims, and this similarity enhances the parallels that can be drawn from the findings.

The three women in this study were selected because they were matched along the following dimensions I had selected: (1) they were white females; (2) they were between the ages of 26 and 28 years old; (3) they were currently or had been married; and (4) they had had a sexual experience with their natural fathers before they were teenagers.

Susan (Subject 1)   1st type

Through contacts with treatment personnel in the Women's Correctional Institution in Milledgeville, Georgia, an offender was located who had had a childhood sexual relationship with her father. The treatment personnel approached the victim about participating in a series of interviews with me for this research. She agreed, and a time was set for weekly interviews to take place at the institution.

I wanted to interview a female offender because there is considerable evidence in the literature to suggest that those who experience an incestuous relationship during childhood are more vulnerable to pathological development in later life (Geiser, 1979) and that a considerable number of victims suffer lasting harm. This seems to be particularly true when the sexual relationship involved the use of force or threats, was of long duration, and the perpetrator was a close family friend or relative. Incest is disorganizing in its impact. Victims often demonstrate anxiety, depression, underachievement, somatic or eating disorders, and self-defeating behaviors. Feelings of unworthiness are internalized at an early age. Some victims struggle all their lives to receive the love and nurturing they were deprived of in childhood.

Often the disturbances in later life are evidenced by a history of divorces, institutionalizations, or behavioral disorders such as prostitution and drug or alcohol abuse. There also appears to be a tendency toward repeated victimization in adult life, such as being battered, victims of rape, or running away. It has been implied that a prevalent reaction is acts of behavioral deviance (Gruber, Jones & Freeman, 1982).

Judy (Subject 2)   2nd type

Considerable evidence is mounting that some females who experience incest in childhood consider themselves permanently injured and therefore seek therapy (James & Meyerding, 1977). Frequently these women report low self-esteem, sexual dysfunctions, depression, guilt, shame, feelings of isolation, and mistrust of both males and females.

Judy was a member of an ongoing therapy group for women who had experienced an incestuous relationship during childhood. She was the one selected from the eight members of the group because she was willing to tell her story, and also because she most closely matched the demographic variables of the other two participants.

3rd type

Nancy (Subject 3)

Finally, there is evidence that some females who were sexually molested by their fathers in childhood consider themselves "well adjusted" and not in need of therapy. Indeed, there are even advocates who believe that early sexual experience with one's father can be truly beneficial for the child (Ramey, 1979).

If this is true, it is reasonable to assume that many victims have been able to put the incestuous relationship behind them and have gone on to live "normal" lives, never seeking therapy and never in violation of the law severely enough to be incarcerated.

Therefore, I placed an advertisement in the newspaper for a willing subject, who met the criteria, to select herself for the study.

Several women responded to the newspaper advertisement. However, none of them was found satisfactory for participation in this study. Two women had had a childhood sexual relationship with their foster fathers rather than with their natural fathers. One woman called and agreed to participate once the study was explained to her; however, she wanted to be paid for her life story. A final call came from a woman who decided that she did not want to participate once she learned that I myself had not been sexually abused by my father. She felt that I could not understand what she had experienced.

After several weeks, it was determined that a newspaper advertisement would not result in my third participant. Soon thereafter a fellow doctoral student said she thought she had a friend who met the criteria for the study and who might be willing to participate. She contacted her friend, who then agreed to be interviewed.

In anticipation of stressful memories being renewed as a result of the interviews, I offered free support therapy, should the need arise, to all three women.

Field Experience

During the series of interviews, the interview guide was not rigidly adhered to, nor was the intent such. My focus was to learn about the women's private psychological processes, such as thoughts, feelings, and the way each viewed who she was and how she got that way. The guide provided a framework within which additional questions could be developed; the sequence of the questions was sometimes changed, and decisions were made concerning which information to pursue in greater detail. Through continual interaction, omissions were elaborated and filled in and refinements brought about. Thus, each life history began to take shape.

Standard open-ended questions had the advantage of allowing me to respond to expressions of uncertainty, to clarify what was being sought, to request additional information, and to elicit fuller, more individualized statements of each woman's thoughts and feelings.

My practice was to follow up on responses by gently probing, reflecting, or following the subject's lead in whatever direction she was taking. The purpose of each interview was to record as completely and impartially as possible the interviewee's perspective.

I conducted each of the interviews. With the exception of Susan, the offender, the interviews took place in a familiar context chosen by the woman. Each session was tape-recorded. This permitted me to be more attentive to the interviewee and also allowed for extensive observations and notes to be written.

Field Experience with Susan

The weekly interviews with Susan covered a two-month period. Approximately twenty-five hours of taped interviews were obtained.

Susan agreed to be a participant after revealing to her counselor at the Women's Institution that "something had gone on" between her and her father. The counselor asked if she would be willing to be interviewed for this study, and she said, "yes," in hopes that such interviews might help her "sort out things in her life."

When I first met Susan, she admitted that she had fully expected me to tell her that she is "crazy" or "that there is something bad wrong" with her. She seemed genuinely surprised and pleased when she realized that these interviews were to be nonjudgmental and that she could use the time to gain some insight into the patterns of her behavior that contributed to her felony convictions and repeated incarcerations.

During our first interview, Susan was very self-conscious about her appearance because she had recently had all of her upper teeth pulled. When she spoke it was barely above a whisper, with her eyes cast to the floor and a hand covering her mouth. She was extremely difficult to hear, and she rarely smiled. However, after an initial introductory period, she visibly seemed to relax and became much freer with her responses to the questions. Early in the first session, she described becoming pregnant by her father when she was fourteen years old. She seemed genuinely surprised when I showed no negative reaction. It was almost as if she felt she had to test the elasticity of our relationship to see if her "secret" would discourage me from returning.

Revealing this secret and being accepted led Susan to tell the rest of her life story willingly. The initial interview lasted approximately four hours and probably would have lasted well into the night had Susan not been called back to her living quarters for the evening count and dinner.

By the second interview, Susan had relaxed and was eager to tell more of her life experiences. She spoke freely of what others might consider very sensitive material, such as the daughter by her father that she bore when she was fifteen, her incarcerations, the adoption of her children, her drug and alcohol abuse, her life as a prostitute, and her exploring bisexual and lesbian relationships. It became more important to put these events in a different perspective in her life, to stop wallowing in guilt and shame, and to make some realistic plans for her future.

Compared to the other two women in this study, Susan required the most actual questioning. At the beginning of each weekly session, Susan would arrive with questions reflecting that she had been thinking about material discussed the previous week. She often had factual questions, such as, "How does one get pregnant?"

During the course of the interviews, I saw a physical change take place in Susan. When we first met, she wore little make-up, rarely curled her hair, and almost never made eye contact or smiled. As the weeks went by, she seemed to take more care with her appearance. She began wearing make-up, had her hair stylishly cut, and started polishing her fingernails. When I commented that I liked the bleach cut out of her hair, she smiled and said, "Yeah, I have decided to just be myself."

Field Experience with Judy

Judy was one of the original members of an ongoing therapy group that I co-lead for women who had had an incestuous experience. We had known each other for approximately two years at the time of the interviews.

Since Judy's second husband was at home during the evenings, she suggested that perhaps it would be better for her to come to my home for the interviews. This was not an attempt to hide anything from her husband, but rather because their apartment was small, and she worried that his movements and talking might interfere with the taping of our sessions. At the time of these interviews a mutual respect and friendship had been established between us. There were four interview sessions with Judy, each lasting approximately three to four hours.

These interviews were the most relaxed of the three women's. There was laughing and joking and not the seriousness that colored Susan's interviews. Early in the interview process, however, I became aware of the need not to second-guess Judy's answers, since much of the material had been brought up and discussed at length in the therapy group meetings.

During the interviews, Judy was in the process of terminating her weekly participation in the therapy group. She was anxious to continue with her part-time job in home cosmetic sales and to pursue her master's degree in special education. She felt she no longer needed the weekly support of the group. While she was eager to develop other areas of her life, she was ambivalent about leaving the group and felt guilty about deserting the other members, as she had been active since the group's inception.

However, she did keep in frequent contact with two of the other three original members. The three of them have developed deep, personal friendships. She and her husband had also recently transferred their church membership and had become involved in activities with couples their own age through the church. Judy was anxious to build up the income she made from the home cosmetic sales business she had started and hoped to be able to pursue this field full time.

The cosmetic company had an incentive program, and if a quota was reached, a "Perfect Start" pin was awarded. While Judy described the pin as a "dumb little pin," she had decided to push to reach her quota and receive the pin. She said that earning the pin would mean, "I can do it! And, that's important!"

Field Experience with Nancy

Nancy was found through a mutual friend. When she was initially approached by the friend, she was a little reluctant to participate because she did not think that the sexual experience with her father had had any long-term consequences. She felt that she therefore might not have anything to offer the study. She did, however, agree to participate on the one condition that she be allowed to read the finished study.

Nancy invited me into her home for the interview. She was friendly, warm, and outgoing. A rapport was easily and quickly developed. Her home is located in a middle-class suburb of a large city. Large yards and lots of trees give the appearance of a peaceful, comfortable neighborhood. We sat in the living room overlooking their back yard. Throughout the afternoon, the family puppy chased squirrels across the yard and up trees. The telephone rang frequently. There were lots of children's toys scattered around the floor. The home had a sense of comfortableness.

There was a lot of laughter throughout the afternoon. Nancy had many of her own questions about the other two women in the study, as well as about my experiences as a therapist with individual clients and a therapy group for women who had been sexually abused as children. She was curious to learn whether she were like the others.

Nancy is very animated when she speaks. Her hands and arms move constantly. Frequently, she would stop in midsentence and ask me if I were getting the material I needed. One question generally elicited a rather long, detailed response from Nancy, so fewer questions were needed than with the other two women.

During the afternoon, Nancy's nine-month-old daughter, Monica, woke up from her nap. We took a break in the interview to allow Monica to become acquainted with me. She smiled frequently and did not display the least hesitation in coming over to me. She was intrigued with the tape recorder and cried when she could not play with it. She spent the rest of the afternoon in the living room and went from playing with her toys and the puppy to pulling record albums off a shelf. Her presence not only allowed observation of the mother–daughter interaction, but also allowed Nancy to reflect on the joys and concerns she has for Monica.

Less time was spent with Nancy than with the other two women. The information gained during the one afternoon appeared sufficient.

Analysis of the Data

Each of the taped interviews was subsequently transcribed verbatim, and observations and notes inserted where appropriate. A chapter was written about each woman. These chapters took the form of stories of each life as it has unfolded to date.

The data were then examined for areas that emerged as common to all three participants. The process of analytic induction was used to examine the emergent patterns, themes, and categories of data. Erik Erikson's theory of psychosocial stages of development was used to provide the perspective of simultaneous comparison of data across instances in which they occurred (Erikson, 1950).

Limitations of the Study

It is recognized that limitations will be encountered in any study involving human subjects. The following specific limitations should be noted by the reader:

1. The results of this phenomenological study cannot be generalized to all women who experienced a sexual relationship with their fathers during childhood.
2. The data on Judy, the participant in the ongoing therapy group, may be contaminated by the personal relationship we have.
3. There is the possibility of my biases creeping in, although an attempt was made to control this by use of taped interview sessions.
4. All three women were volunteers, which may limit the generalization of the results of this study.

5. Each of the life histories was a retrospective portrait with all the simplifications and distortions that might occur in an adult's memory of childhood.

6. This book is about women who had incestuous relations with their fathers. There is no attempt to examine the long-term effects of other incestuous relationships, such as father–son, mother–daughter, mother–son, or sister–brother.

4
Susan's Life

S usan is an attractive Caucasian mother of four. She is four feet, eleven inches tall and weighs approximately 106 pounds. She has short brown hair, which is streaked with blond. She speaks with such a soft voice that one has to lean forward often to hear what she is saying. She chain-smokes and constantly drinks cups of black coffee. These habits take the place of the alcohol she consumed on a daily basis when she was on the streets. Susan is an alcoholic.

Unless one notices her tattoos—a cross on her right pinkie finger, an *SR* on her left upper arm, and a *JD* on her left ankle—at first glance one might mistake her for a suburban housewife instead of a convicted felon. She is currently serving time in a women's prison for her third conviction. Susan is twenty-eight years old.

Susan's Childhood

Susan is the third oldest of the fifteen children in her family of origin. She has an older brother and an older sister. Her father, an enlisted man, made a career of the army. He was frequently out of the home either on temporary duty or for training exercises. He served in both Korea and Vietnam.

Susan's mother was a housewife and was never legally employed outside of the home. According to Susan, her mother was an "army whore" who prostituted herself on a regular basis and moved other men into the home when the father was gone. Of the fifteen children, only six were actually Susan's father's.

I: Who fathered the other children?

S: Different men. One of them belonged to my daddy's best friend. My daddy left home and told my mother that if she messed around with his friend he would kill them both. She messed around with him.

I: How did your father know it wasn't his child?

S: I guess she told him. Or he knew her pretty well. Every time he went on duty somewhere she would move another man in with us. One time my daddy had a thirty-day leave and he came home unexpectedly. When he came in, he slept on the couch. My mom had some friend with her in their bedroom. She used to tell us kids that these men wanted to look at the bedroom furniture to see about buying it. We was young and didn't know no better. Now that I know what she was doing in there with them, I hate her.

Being one of the oldest children, it often fell upon Susan to take care of her younger siblings. When she talks about her early years, the predominant theme is one of sadness and grief for the childhood she never was allowed to experience. A dominant memory is of physical beatings. She remembers staying out of the house a lot while her mother entertained male friends.

S: I played outside a lot. Some days I would write "I hate Mother" in the dirt in the yard. My sister would tell on me, and my mother would come chase me around with a broom handle. That is what she would whip me with. A broom handle or three or four switches tied together.

Frequent beatings were also administered to Susan and her siblings by her father. Susan does not think either parent had to be drinking when they beat the kids. She is puzzled why such seemingly little things set them off on a "rampage" against the children.

S: When my daddy was home, he would get real angry with us kids. He wouldn't be like most people and sit down and talk with their kids. Like if a kid comes home from school with a bad report card or homework to do that they don't understand, most parents would sit down and try to help their kid. Not my daddy. He would get mad if we didn't learn something or if our report cards weren't good enough, and he would hit us. He didn't use no broom handle or switches; he would hit us with his fists.

Susan's maternal grandfather is the only other significant adult she mentions when talking about her childhood. He cut grass for a living and frequently took her with him. As a child, she viewed these excursions as special times because they not only got her out of the house and away from her mother, but also because her grandfather always bought her an ice cream cone on the way home. Maturity has given her a different perspective on these afternoons.

S: Cutting grass was the only kind of work my grandfather ever did. He would buy me an ice cream cone if I would pull off my clothes. It would be just the two of us in his truck. I didn't think it was wrong. Then one day he tried it [intercourse] with me, but I don't know what happened. It's like he was too big. Instead, I started crying and he quit. I was five then. The thing about it is he would bribe me. He gave me the ice cream which we didn't have at home. At the time I didn't know what he was doing, but now I know. He would look at me without my clothes on, masturbate, and get off every time.

When Susan was asked to sum up her reflections on her childhood, she sat quietly for a minute and then replied:

S: I can't remember nothing good about my childhood. One Christmas I remember I was sick and didn't want to get out of bed. My mother wanted me to get up. She whipped me and then gave me a doll. I treated that doll like she did me. I hated it.

While Susan was in elementary school, the family frequently came to the attention of legal authorities and social service agencies. The first contact with the legal system came when Susan's father had her older sister sent to a reform school.

S: I am not sure how old I was, but one time my father tried something sexual with my older sister. She stabbed him. He had her sent off to reform school. When she got out, she married a black dude and moved to Texas. I have lost track of her.

Once this sister was out of the house, the father then turned to Susan for sexual companionship.

S: He started when I was around eight. Once my dad picked me to be with, he would be real sweet to me. My mom started calling me the "black sheep" and all that stuff. I blame my mother. I figure if she would have given it to him, he wouldn't have come to me for it or to my sister. But then I think, my God, look how many times she gave it to him. She had fifteen kids. I didn't want sex with my daddy. I just wanted someone to love me. I did not want someone to beat me.

It was at this time that Susan started what was to become a pattern of running away from home and being placed in foster homes. She was eventually declared a habitual runaway and was sent to a reform school when she was thirteen.

The first time she ran away she was eight years old. She says she had left home to go spend the night at a friend's house when the police picked her up. This proved to be the first of what would eventually become many nights spent in jails.

The family also came to the attention of social service workers through school personnel. Although Susan now sees that this would have been a possible way for her and her siblings to escape their home and parents, nothing ever came of these investigations.

S: The court workers used to come to our house all of the time. My mother would beat us kids. She would chase us with a broom handle or anything else she could get her hands on. I came close to getting stabbed by her one time. She was arguing with a man after they had been drinking a lot. I opened the front door. She threw a knife at it. It missed and got stuck in the wall. But then she got real mad and beat me. . . .

When we went to school, the teachers would report us to the office because of all of the bruises. When the social workers came to the house, she would lie. No one really seemed to care. My dad was in Korea then. I told them the truth, but they didn't believe me. When they met my mom, that was end of it. She is real pretty, and she can make a man believe anything. . . .

One time I told a judge, "My mom sells herself." I laid it all out for him. A whole bunch of stuff that had gone on at home. My mom just looked at me and said, "Now, Susan, you ought to be ashamed of yourself. You know I don't do that." So the judge told her that I just needed to have a good paddling. Of course my mom would go right along with that. She was a great con. She could make a man believe anything. I think I could have killed her that day. I really hated her deeply.

For the next two years, although Susan continued to run away, she stayed in the home. When she was ten, the court took her out of the home and placed her in what was to be a long succession of foster families. She was glad to be out of her mother's reach, but had difficulty adjusting to the different homes. She did not like being told what to do, and she did not like the feeling of being pitied by the foster parents.

S: In the foster families, they would give them my background. It was like they really pitied me. I remember some of them [foster parents] would get together at night and I would be lying in bed, and they would be talking about me. They would say things like, "This little girl . . . poor thing, she is so little and defenseless," or "I could just kill her parents for what they have done to her." They were all feeling pity for me and I just didn't like that. . . .

I did have one family that I really liked though. He was a preacher. He would take me around as his daughter. We went to church, and he would tell people I was his daughter. I was not used to that. I did not know how to act when someone acted like they loved me or was proud of me. I loved him. But then his wife started trying to put restrictions on me . . . "You can't do this or you can't do that." She made me mad so I just ran away. I ruined it.

Between foster families, Susan was returned to her own family. Her attendance in school was sporadic because of all her moving around. She remembers that she liked school and saw it as a way to get away from her mother. Susan liked history, but says she barely passed math and science. She regrets not trying harder in school and at least graduating from high school.

Susan related an increasing sense of secrecy in her life as she grew older. She did not feel she could trust either of her parents, and when she tried to go to the authorities through the school personnel, she was not believed. She never felt friends would be able to accept her if they knew what was going on in her family, so she learned to keep things to herself and to stay away from home as much as possible.

When Susan was in the sixth grade, her mother taught her to shoplift. This brought her to the attention of the legal system once again.

S: Whenever my sister and I would stay at home from school, my mother would have us shoplift for her. She taught us how to do it. Whenever she wanted something new, she would just tell us what she wanted; we would go get it for her. I don't know why we done it, but we did. We took dresses, shoes, everything. One time she even told me she wanted the flowers off a lady's porch, and I went and got them for her. Even now sometimes I steal just to see if I can do it and get away with it.

Sexual Relationships within the Family

Although it was never mentioned, in retrospect, Susan thinks it is possible that her maternal grandfather and her mother had had a sexual relationship. She feels that her mother probably knew what the grandfather was doing when he took Susan with him to cut grass, and yet she did nothing to stop him.

Susan is also not sure if her father ever had sexual relations with any of her sisters other than the older sister who stabbed him. However, she has vivid memories of the sexual contact that her father initiated with her around this time.

S: I think that my mother pushed him into it. She would drag home anyone she could. Excuse my language, but she was an "army whore." When my daddy came home and she had someone else in their bed, he would just sleep on the sofa. Why do you think he would do that? He never said anything; he just went to sleep on the couch. I know I would turn cold with hatred if I came in and found my husband with another woman. . . .

I am not sure when it started—when I was around eight, I guess, because that is when I started running away. My daddy would wait until my mom went somewhere and then he would run the rest of the kids out of the house. He would take me into the bedroom. I don't think anyone else knew what he was doing. At first he would just look at me and then he would masturbate or have me masturbate him. Then he wanted me to take him in my mouth. I have always thought that was nasty, but he made me do it. He used to threaten me if I told anyone, but he never beat me when we were having sex. I never told anyone. I think my mom knew, though, she had to. It just saved her from having to have sex with my daddy. . . .

I have a piece of skin hanging down there [between her legs] now, kinda like a man. I feel funny about it. When I was nine and went to the hospital, the doctor said it was because someone *way* too big had tried to enter me. It done something to me down there. I don't really remember exactly what happened. Even today if it gets irritated, it bothers me. . . .

After they took me out of our home, I was put in a foster home. I think that is about the time my parents got a divorce. I know we never all lived together again. I guess my mother just got tired of all of us. After my daddy left the last time, she took two of my brothers, gave them a box of saltines, put them on the side of the road, and told them, "Now go find yourself a home." . . .

Anyway, after that they took all of my brothers and sisters away and put them in foster homes. I don't know where any of them are now.

When she was thirteen, Susan was sent to reform school. Once she was released, she had nowhere to live, so she sought out her father, preferring him to her mother.

S: My father lived in an apartment and seemed glad for me to come live with him. He always told me that he loved me. We got along okay for a while. One day while he was at work, a neighbor asked me if I was his wife. I told her that I was his daughter. Then I found out that he had been telling people we were married. I loved him, and at thirteen, I really wanted to be *something*. I had even thought of following him into the army. Then after he started messing with me [this time] it didn't seem to matter any more. . . .

My room in his apartment looked like a story book. I had a stereo and every kind of doll you can imagine. It was beautiful. He gave me lots of gifts. We were real happy together, but then he expected sex in return for the gifts. . . .

One night he gave me some liquor. It was good. It didn't taste like liquor, and I got drunk. That night was the first time we had intercourse. I guess I passed out or something because I don't remember exactly what happened. The next day I woke up with blood all over me. He had gotten up and gone to work already. Just the two of us were living there so I got up and cleaned myself up. At first, I wasn't sure what had happened, but when he came in that night, he wanted sex again. I knew what it was. . . .

He always told me that I was a good lover and I would make somebody a fantastic wife one day. He always said he loved me. For a while I guess I went crazy or something; I thought I loved him like a husband. We got along okay for a while; I thought I really loved him. He would go to work, and I would stay home and clean or watch television. Here I was fourteen, and he was in his forties. It was kinda crazy.

This relationship lasted for several more months. It was the first time in her life that Susan remembers ever feeling a sense of love and security. However, it was to be short-lived. The arrival of her father's nineteen-year-old Korean wife changed the relationship between father and daughter and changed the living arrangements.

Her father had married this girl on his tour of duty in Korea. It had taken several months for her to arrive in the United States. She never knew of the relationship between her husband and his daughter.

S: I liked my daddy's wife okay. She wasn't that much older than me. She did not talk much English. We didn't have much to do with each other. . . .

About the same time she came I met a guy and wanted to go out and get a Coke with him and all. My daddy didn't want me to go out with boys. I don't know why he cared; he was married and his wife was right there with him. Anyway, every time I went out there was a big fight. He said he hated to see me throw my life away on boys. . . .

What is funny is that I didn't have sex with any of the boys I dated. I can take sex or leave it. Anyway, a short time later I found out that I was pregnant, and I knew it was my daddy's. I hadn't been with anyone else. He did not know whose it was and he wanted me to get an abortion, but I don't believe in those. So, I left. . . .

Now when I think about my daddy there are so many questions I would like to ask him like, "Why did he do this or that?" I don't guess I will ever know why.

Susan's Marriages

Once she left her father's apartment, Susan went to live with a family she had met. In a short time she met Dan, an offshore oilman who was five years her senior, and married him. She was fifteen and he was twenty at the time. He did not know she was pregnant. Although Susan did not love Dan, she was looking for a "place to live and a father for my child." To this day, Dan thinks the daughter is his flesh and blood.

S: At first we did not get legally married because I was not old enough and my daddy would not sign for me. Dan was Cajun and my daddy thought that meant he was black. He wouldn't sign because he hates blacks. We didn't legally get married, but we signed everything Mr. and Mrs. After a while we did get legally married though. We lived with his family because we didn't have no place else to go.

Susan describes the pregnancy as normal. She had the baby in a charity hospital and remembers being very frightened. She says she never remembers really wanting to have the child or feeling any sense of love for the child.

S: It may be wrong for me to say this, but I never wanted her like a mother should want her baby. After she was born, every time I looked at her, I saw my daddy. People said she looks exactly like me, but I just saw my daddy in her face.

The marriage to Dan lasted only a brief time. Susan has very little to say about the time they were married. However, she remembers the ugliness that surrounded their divorce and subsequent custody fight.

S: Everything was okay until the same old thing started happening. My husband caught his daddy messing with me. I didn't want nothing like that with him, but he wanted to have sex with me. He was always trying to sneak a feel. Dan got real mad. He said if I didn't dress and look like I did, his daddy would never have tried anything like that. I happen to think that running around in shorts and a halter top at sixteen years old is pretty normal. Anyway, they all blamed me for what his daddy done. They threw me out.

Susan went to live with a woman she had met previously. She took a job in a truck stop as a waitress. She and Dan had bitter arguments over custody of their daughter. Susan felt alone and helpless in fighting Dan and his family for custody.

S: One night Dan came around to see me. We was arguing over the custody again. He told me he wanted to take me for a ride. We went out on a dirt road, and after a while he got tired of fighting with me and told me to get out and to walk back home. I got out and was walking back to town, and in a few minutes this car with six black dudes came up. They picked me up and said they would give me a ride back to town. Dan hated blacks, but I never had anything against them. Anyway, the next thing I knew, they were offering me wine. I told them I didn't want none, but they held me and poured it down my throat. The next thing I knew, I am on the ground with them holding me down, pouring wine down my throat and taking my clothes off. I tried to get away, but there was six of them. They got me good and drunk. They got what they wanted. All six of them raped me. I have always thought that Dan set them up to do that, but I can't say for sure. When we went to court, he told the judge that I had sex with black men. I tried to tell the judge what happened, but he didn't believe me. The judge gave my husband the custody of our little girl.

A short time after the divorce, Susan tried to kidnap her daughter. She did not succeed in this attempt and was sent to reform school for four months. After she was released, Dan told her that he wanted her out of their lives altogether. He has never allowed Susan to write, call, or come see their daughter.

S: I haven't seen my little girl for ten years. She looked a lot like me the last time I saw her. I have never said this before, but when I get out [of prison] I am going to go and get her. I figure when I get out this time, I will have my life straight. Dan won't let me communicate with them, but I think if I go to the state they live in, I can find them. He has a lot of relatives. I would like to get to know her. If she is doing anything like drugs, prostitution, or anything, I am going to try to talk to her. Oh, I mean I am not going to come up to her and say, "Hey, I am your mom" or nothing like that. But after we get to know each other, I may tell her. I am scared because she might be doing wrong. She might be a whore, and that would hurt me. I would have to kill Dan for letting her go like that.

It was at this time in her life that Susan first started drinking heavily. She was again working in a truck stop and living with an old woman who had befriended her. She says she often got so drunk that she did not know where she was. This was the first hint that she had alcoholism, but she paid little attention. She drank simply to drown her sorrows.

She met her second husband while she was getting drunk and hanging out nightly in bars. This marriage lasted for one and a half years and produced her first son.

S: My second husband would see me in the bar drunk, and he would take me to his mother's house and take care of me. I would go back to the bar the next day when he went to work and it would start all over again. I just didn't care about anything after my divorce. He would come and take me to sober up. He tried to get me to talk, but I wouldn't. He worked offshore in the oil field. He'd come home and I'd be off to the bar again. Finally one night I told him about my little girl. He said we could fight for her if that was what I wanted. He took me to see her, but my ex-husband wouldn't let us in. I don't know if he was just jealous of my boyfriend or what. Anyway, he called the police. My boyfriend left when he saw the police coming. They told me to go on home and not start any trouble. I left. . . .

I forgave him for leaving me, and we eventually got married. Then he started wanting to go out by himself. He started messing around with other women. I had had our son by then and didn't know what to do. I thought about killing myself. I was ready to leave this world. I gave the lady next door the baby and told her I was going to end it all. She called her preacher. He came and talked to me. When my husband came in, I told him I wanted to start going to church. He said no. If I wanted to go, go, but he was not going. Seems like in my life when I have wanted to do something like that, someone I wanted to share it with would always say no. So, I finally left him while he was at work one day and I took the baby.

Susan went to live with a girl she had met in a bar. Shortly afterwards, another man came into her life. He was a mechanic and wanted Susan and her son to come live with him. She was waitressing in another truck stop and had very little money at the time. The prospect of having someone look after her and her son was too attractive to refuse. Although this marriage did not last very long, Susan became pregnant with her second son. She left this man before the child was born.

Homeless and pregnant, Susan decided to return to Alabama in an attempt to find some of her siblings. She went to her maternal grandmother's house and received a hostile reception. This trip proved to be the last contact Susan has had with her immediate family.

> S: I went to Alabama mainly looking for the sister next to me. We had always been close when we was growing up. I went to my grand-mother's house. My mother was living there. So was one of my younger sisters. My mother had prostituted my sister when she was eleven or twelve years old for ten dollars. Can you believe that? Ten dollars! She was fifteen then and already had hit the needle with heroin. It shocked me when I saw her. I couldn't believe it. She had big tits and all. I thought of her as my baby sister still. I got real mad at my mother. Then my grandmother started fighting with me. She said that I was just like my mother. I didn't pay much attention to what she said at first, but then I was real hurt. All of my life I had said I never wanted to be like my mother. But, I guess when you put our lives together I measure right up to her. Like being a prostitute, using drugs, giving up our kids . . . even being right here in prison. . . .
>
> I told them all I never wanted to see them again. And, I never have. I don't know where any of them are. I wouldn't mind seeing my brothers and sisters, but I am not going to look for them.

After leaving Alabama, Susan lived with people she met in bars. Susan and her son moved around frequently. Her second son was delivered in another charity hospital. After his birth, she again found work as a topless dancer and waitress in a nightclub. During this time, she met the man who would become her third husband and the father of her fourth child. He, like her preceding husband, worked as a mechanic. Shortly after moving in with him, she discovered she was pregnant. At first she decided to seek an abortion. However, she changed her mind once she actually got to the abortion clinic. She delivered her fourth child, a second daughter.

This marriage lasted for three years and was relatively uneventful in Susan's mind. She felt she could talk with this husband and had hopes that maybe this marriage would work out and that finally she would be part of a "family."

> S: Things were going okay for us until there was this family reunion. I kept saying I didn't want to go, but my husband made me go. All of

these people kept coming up to me and saying, "Oh, I am your so and so," or "Who is your mother?" When I would tell them who my mother was they would say I looked just like her. I ain't never seen any of them in my life, and they all seemed to know me. I got to talking to some of them, and it turned out that me and my husband were third cousins. I don't know what happened, if it was me or what. It was just the thought of us being related like that. I never wanted to be around him any more. It seemed wrong to me to have sex with him. I left.

At twenty-two, with three children to support (one child was in the custody of her first husband) and no high school diploma or vocational training, Susan turned to prostitution to support herself and her children. In 1977, she was arrested and sent to prison for the first time. Because she had no immediate family, the children were each placed in a foster home. After completing her sentence, Susan returned and regained custody of her children. However, she and her caseworker from the social service agency were in constant conflict, and Susan felt the woman was "always on my case."

S: When I got out and got the children back, the caseworker just kept after me. The state said I couldn't take care of them. Seems like everything was coming down on me at one time. I didn't know what to do. The caseworker said she knew a Christian lady who would be willing to take all three of them and give them a Christian home. I was drinking and didn't have a job. I thought about it and thought it might be the best thing for them, so I signed the papers. I told them I didn't want their names changed, but I don't know if they did change them or not. That was five years ago, and I haven't seen or heard from them since. The records are sealed so I really don't know where they are. I hope that they are okay. I think about them. It leaves a pain. Sometimes when I would get to drinking, I would get in my car and say I was going to get them, but I don't know where they are. I still have pictures of the two boys. I carry them in my wallet on the streets, but in here I have them in my Bible.

Susan's Current Boyfriend

Susan's current boyfriend, Mike, is a 56-year-old construction worker. He regularly comes to see her on visiting days at the prison and sends her money every month. He is her only contact with the world outside of the prison walls.

S: I met Mike one time when me and my girlfriend were running away from our probation officer. The police were looking for us, and we was hitchhiking. He and his friend picked us up. I was honest with him. I told him if he would help me, I would help him. He has stood by me. He has never let me down. He wants to marry me after I get out and his wife dies.

Although Susan is not exactly sure why Mike's wife is confined to a wheelchair, she thinks that the woman is terminally ill. According to what Mike has told her, the doctors do not expect his wife to live much longer. Mike's wife is unaware that Mike visits and sends money to Susan. They have been married for over thirty years and have two children and several grandchildren.

S: At one time I lived with Mike and his wife. I was helping to take care of her because she can't do nothing for herself. I started calling her "Mama" which is something I have never done with anyone. She told everyone, "Susan is the daughter I could never have." We all got along fine. They were like the parents I never had. . . .

This guy came along and messed it all up for me. We were dating so Mike's wife would not think anything was going on between me and Mike. One night this guy took some guns from the house. She thought I was in on it. She made me leave. I thought the world of her. Mike says it is best that I don't see her again before she dies. He says she looks at a card I sent her and cries, but she won't talk about me and she don't want me around. I would like to see her before she dies. I always loved her.

Mike says he wants to marry Susan once she is released from prison. However, this will depend on his wife's death, as he feels he cannot divorce her. Susan says she cares about Mike, but finds she just cannot trust any man. While she is in prison, it is nice to have the visits and spending money Mike provides.

S: I know it's wrong but when I look at a man, I see a dollar sign. I see how I can use him. I go out to hurt a male. I know I am going to do it, too. Like Mike says he loves me and I will say I love him too, but I know I am going to hurt him when I walk out of his life. I know I am not going to marry him when I get back to the streets.

It is not unusual for Susan to be attracted to and involved with males older than she is. However, with Mike there is no sexual attraction. She describes him as "ugly" and says he has "a big belly and not from just drinking beer."

S: I have no desire for him sexually. He knows a lot about me and accepts me for what I am. He knows about me and Cookie [Susan's lesbian lover in prison]. He accepts that. He believes he loves me and I think he does. He used to be a deacon in a church, and he quit going to church so he can come and see me on Sundays. And the preacher lives right behind him, too. . . .

I guess I don't expect a male to be gentle and kind sexually. But Mike is not like most men. I don't let him foreplay with me, and I don't really know why not. He always asks me questions like, "What gets you hot?" and things like that. I will just say, "Nothing . . . just do it." Then he will say, "Your breasts? Is there no certain spot that feels good?" I tell him no, but they do. I lie to him because I don't want him doing no foreplay on me. I just want to get it over with. Now, sometimes I think if he were someone younger that would be different.

I: Sometimes it sounds to me as if Mike is the first man who has taken your feelings into consideration.

S: I guess so. Like he won't get off unless he thinks I have. I will lie to him and say, "Yeah, I did," but I never do. I don't want to hurt him so I lie just to get it over with. . . .

I tell Mike that I will marry him when I get out, but when the time comes, I don't think I will go through with it. But when someone down here [in the prison] makes fun of him and says that he is fat or old, I am ready to fight them. I guess I keep telling him that I love him because I guess I need him. I think he can help to change me. He has begged me to stop drinking when I get out. He says that if I get into any more trouble, that's it. He begs me not to drink and get into trouble. He is good to me—there is just nothing physical. Maybe we just started the relationship off wrong. He would ask me, "Do you like this or that?" I would say, "No, just go ahead and do it." So maybe it is my fault the way I started it out . . . not getting off and then lying about it. . . .

When he came down here last week he told me, "I tried to have sex with Mama and she can't do it." That really made me sad. He told me that he thought he loved her more than he could ever love anyone, but since he's met me he is not so sure any more. He realizes that he doesn't love her as much as he thought. But he told me he can't leave her. I told him that I don't want him to. I couldn't live with that.

I wouldn't want him if he left her. I would be scared that the next one that come along, he would leave me.

Susan is obviously confused about her feelings for Mike. He appears to like her just as she is. He has encouraged her to stop dyeing her hair and wearing such heavy make-up. It is very difficult for Susan to accept his love and affection because there is no sex involved in their relationship while she is incarcerated, and yet he continues to be supportive.

> S: I don't know why I hurt people who are good to me. Mike shows me he loves me by the things he is doing. I had him buy Christmas presents for me to give to the girls down here. I have had him send money and things to the girls that don't have no family. He don't ever question me, he just sends whatever I ask him to. He sends me a money order for $20 every week. He works hard for his money, and I know that Mama don't know he sends me money, so it is hard for him but he never lets me down. I just don't want to go to bed with him.

Susan's Common-Law Husband

In between Susan's three husbands, there were many men in her life. One who particularly stands out in her mind is her common-law husband, Bill. They were living together with his mother until he was killed in 1982. He had been in prison also and was on parole at the time. He was divorced and had one grown daughter who visited Susan and Bill regularly. Susan got along well with both Bill's mother and his daughter. Susan now thinks that Bill may have been the "love of her life." Once again, she thought she was finally going to feel a part of a family.

The shock of Bill's death is just now beginning to wear off enough for Susan to begin mourning his murder. The trouble, which eventually ended when he was murdered, began when he was laid off his job around Christmas of the previous year. He had been unable to find other employment.

> S: Bill and I had a lot in common. He had been in prison and had experienced different things when he was younger just like me. When we first lived together, it was like a friendship I guess. Then it grew into love. To him, I was beautiful. We shared a lot of things. I could talk to him like I never could to no other man before. One night I got drunk and I told him about my kids. He told me what I said the next day because I didn't remember nothing. He said, "Susan, you know, you have had a rough life." He seemed to understand and love me

anyway. He accepted me even knowing about things I had been through. He also told me things about his life that he had never told no one, not even his wife. . . .

Our favorite thing was to sit in front of the TV, drink a beer, and watch the football games. We did a lot of things together. It seemed to matter to him what I thought and what I wanted to do. We even went to the grocery store together. We shared everything. To him I was a *somebody*.

The events leading to Bill's death are still very painful for Susan to think about and to discuss. She falls into frequent silences and gets teary-eyed, but never quite loses control when describing the night he was killed.

S: I don't know, sometimes I think God is punishing me too much. Bill is the only man I have ever really loved. Last Christmas when he was out of work, he was really upset because he couldn't buy his mom, me, or his daughter any presents. One night he just wanted to go out and get some drugs. When we got to the dealer's house, Bill wanted me to stay in the van and keep it cranked. I didn't know what he had in mind but I told him, "No. No way. I am coming in with you." Besides, I didn't know how to drive a straight shift. So finally he said, "Okay, just leave it running and come on."

When the dealer's wife went out of the room to get the "stuff," Bill came out with a gun to rob the guy. It was crazy. I did not know he had even thought of doing it. He was so much shorter than the dealer, that the dealer just took the gun away and shot Bill in the head. I don't know if I just couldn't believe it or what, but I just stood there. I had a knife in the back of my pants, but I couldn't think of it. I was on probation, and all I could see was coming back to prison. Bill's brains were blown away. He was bleeding to death in front of me, and I couldn't do nothing. I couldn't cry or nothing. The dealer told me to get on the couch. I really didn't care if he shot me or not. Bill was dying on the floor in front of me and I just sat there and looked. The police came. I told them I had tried the robbery because I didn't want Bill's mother to think her son was an armed robber as she buried him. I didn't care what they did to me. I just couldn't cry. I never have cried about it. Sometimes even now I find myself talking to him. I miss him every day.

For reasons Susan is not aware of, no one was ever charged with Bill's murder, nor was the drug dealer ever arrested, although the police found the drugs when they came and searched the house. After Bill's death, Susan continued to live with his mother, but grew increasingly depressed and suicidal. She also began to drink heavily again.

> S: I was real depressed after Bill died. I didn't want to go on living without Bill. So, one day, I just got drunk and cut my wrists. I drove my car into a telephone pole and tried to kill myself. The police arrested me for DUI. Since I was already on parole, they revoked me and sent me here to prison again. I was in real bad shape. I just wanted to die. I was tired. I kept thinking, "Why keep going?"

Because the interviews took place around the Christmas holidays—exactly one year after Bill was killed—Susan was feeling extremely depressed. The idea of being depressed scared her because she was not sure what she might do to herself. For the first time, she began to cry about Bill's death and mourn his passing and their lost relationship. She found that she did not feel like going to dinner many nights, but preferred to stay by herself in her room, lie on her bed, listen to music on the radio, and cry.

> S: Sometimes I think I blame Bill for my being here again. A lot of times when I am in my room by myself, I'll talk to him as if he was there too. I say things like, "Bill, if it weren't for you, I wouldn't be here again. You went and died and let me come back to prison. You sorry so and so." Sometimes I think if he had lived, I wouldn't have ever been back here again.

Susan has not kept in contact with Bill's mother over this past year, but has often wondered how she was getting along and how Bill's death was affecting her. The state gives each inmate two Christmas cards with free postage each year, and Susan chose to send one of the cards to Bill's mother.

> S: I didn't have no one else to send the card to so I sent it to Bill's mother. Now I am worried if I done the right thing. I don't know what kind of shape she is in. I probably shouldn't have done it. But I wanted her to know that I miss him, too. I told her how I was feeling. She drinks too much. She had two sons, and now both of them are in the ground. I am not sure she can talk about Bill's death. I don't like to hurt other people, but I wanted her to know how I feel and that I was thinking about her.

An area of the relationship with Bill that Susan still has a lot of questions about is sex. Although she says she enjoyed the sexual relationship with Bill more than she had with previous men, she finds herself questioning whether she is "normal" in a sexual sense.

S: I like my sex rough. I figure it goes back to my daddy with all of his threats, and when those black dudes raped me.

I: I am not sure what you mean by "rough."

S: Kinky. Hitting don't bother me none. Like usually men pop me around a little or something like that when we have sex. It feels better to me when it hurts. I like rough foreplay. . . .

One time I let Bill talk me into letting him tie me to the bed when we was going to have sex. I had heard a lot about that so I decided I would try it. He tied me up, and it was okay. When he was done, he went to cut the ropes off, and he pulled out a knife. I panicked. I don't mind no gun, but a knife scares me. I thought he was going to force me to have oral sex or something. I remembered what he told me once about the little girl. She was standing on the street corner trying to be a prostitute. She kept making a play for him so he finally took it. She was talking about doing this and that for him, but when it came down to it, she would say "no." So, he forced her. He said that little girl went home and never did come back out again!

Susan also appears to be confused about the distinction between love or affection and sex. She admits that often just having a "warm body" next to her in the bed helps to blot out her intense loneliness. Because she dropped out of school in the eighth grade, she has never had any formal sex education, and her knowledge about her body, a male's body, and adult sexual relations is almost nonexistent.

S: I wonder sometimes if some of my problems go back to my grand-father when he would bribe me for sex. I do that now with men. I get what they give me, and the sex is just a by-product. Maybe I can learn to quit using men. But really, I can take sex or leave it. I used to think a woman had to have a climax to get pregnant, but now I am not so sure. I have had four kids, and I really don't know what a climax is. I find that when I go to bed with a man now, I pretend to like it when really I am not. I don't know if I ever have a climax or not. I used to think something was wrong with me, like I was cold or something. . . .

You reckon the way my daddy done me has made me scared or some-thing? Like scared to let loose and trust a man? Not let my feelings out, but just keep them locked up like I have been doing all of my life?

Susan sees the relationship she had with her father as a major obstacle in her attempts to talk to people about sex. She says even today she thinks she was crazy at the time of that relationship. She is afraid that either people will laugh at her because she knows so little about sexuality, or they will not understand how anyone gets into a sexual relationship with her own father and therefore will think she is "dirty" or "perverted." She is also afraid that people will not want to be around her if they know about her past.

> S: I feel weird sometimes. I know there are other people who have been with their fathers sexually, but a fifteen-year-old? I don't see no other fifteen-year-old laying down with their father. A man can go with me now, and I feel dirty. I don't know why. Oral sex makes me sick, too. I have only tried it with my daddy and Bill. But it's nasty, and I don't like it. Some people probably will think I am crazy, but that is just how I feel.

Susan's Relationship with Cookie

During her second incarceration for concurrent sentences on prostitution and car theft, Susan met a girl nicknamed Cookie. Their friendship continued once they were both released from prison. At different times they have lived with each other. They have been lovers. Susan frequently has her boyfriend, Mike, send Cookie money, since Cookie's family has given up on her and refuses to have any contact with her now that she is locked up again. Cookie is currently serving a fifteen-year sentence for armed robbery.

> S: When I get down, Cookie is the only one I can talk to. She is the only one I can trust. She knows everything about me and what has happened in the past. She accepts and likes me anyway.

> I: Sounds like part of what you like about Cookie is that you have been able to tell her your secrets and she hasn't let you down. The fear you have now is that if you tell anyone else, they won't be able to accept you?

> S: I don't see how they could. I know I am down on myself a lot, but I don't see how people could like me once they know what I have been through. Sometimes I hurt people just to see if I can. Cookie tries to show me love, but I push her away sometimes. Anyway, *she* says I do. She and I have had a sexual relationship and she is like the man. She always asks me the same things a man would. I hurt her feelings when I don't get off. She used to get mad, and say she was just giving up. I would tell her it wasn't her, it was me. She was doing all of the right things, I just couldn't get off. Sometimes when I am in bed with a man, I will think of Cookie. It's stupid.

Susan is very confused about her relationship with Cookie right now. Prior to their current incarcerations, they were living together. They had an argument that supposedly resulted in Cookie taking some drugs and committing the armed robbery. Susan feels responsible for Cookie being in prison again. As a result, Susan buys Cookie cigarettes and soft drinks from the weekly check she receives from Mike. She also frequently asks Mike to send Cookie money, too.

However, while they have been at the women's prison this time, Susan feels she has grown increasingly independent of Cookie. She has begun to question the value of this friendship and question whether she is, in fact, being "used" by Cookie.

Susan and Cookie are not currently involved in a sexual relationship with each other. Susan is trying to sort out her feelings about her sexuality and to decide if perhaps she is bisexual. Cookie, who is living in a different housing unit, is involved in a sexual relationship with a black woman. However, Cookie still expects Susan to share her money and cigarettes with her. This expectation has resulted in several severe arguments.

S: Cookie and me had a fight the other night about her new girlfriend. I told her I just wanted her to be honest with me. She jumped up like she was going to hit me. I told her, "You know pain don't hurt me none, go ahead, hit me." She said, "Susan, you are crazy." Sometimes I think it is Cookie who is keeping me down. She is always saying to me, "Susan, you are crazy," or "Susan, you are sick." Sometimes I feel better when she is just not around.

I: Why does she think you are sick?

S: Because I am not scared of her. She came in here with a name, "I'm bad." She will fly off the handle and hurt you, but I stand up to her. No one else here does that; they are all afraid of her. People will look at me and say, "Susan, you are so little; you better be careful with Cookie." I tell them, "Why should I be afraid? She is just another female. All she is going to do is beat me up." She gets off by hurting people . . . mentally, physically, and emotionally, whatever. . . .

Last night I saw her playing pool, and she looked like she needed someone to talk to. So I went over and asked her if she wanted to talk. She said, "I can deal with it, get out of my face." She said she is going to do the same thing to me that I do to her. She keeps telling me she loves me. Yet, every time we are around each other she don't show nothing but anger. I buy her cigarettes. I have Mike send her money. Her family is all working; they could buy her stuff, but they don't. People around here tell me I am crazy for helping her.

I: Why do you keep helping her?

S: I don't know.

I: One time you said you feel guilty about her being here, is that it?

S: I don't know if that is it or not.

I: Is it because she is the best friend you think you have ever had?

S: I am not sure what it is. We had our good times, but the bad times outweigh them now.

I: Could it be that you find the loving, tender kindness in the sexual relationship with her that you haven't been able to find with a man?

S: I am more comfortable with her than anyone else. One time when we was living together her little brother and I were home alone. She went to work, and he kept trying to make it with me. I finally just quit fighting. Afterwards, I just took off. I didn't want to tell her what he had done. I came back after I got real drunk because I didn't have no place else to go. I told her what he had done. She wanted to know why I didn't tell her about her brother instead of running off. She beat her brother up and said she wouldn't leave us two alone any more. He told her he was in love with me. She told him, "If you love someone, you don't just take what you want."

I: Maybe you are grateful to Cookie for protecting you?

S: Maybe I just keep holding onto her because I haven't found anyone else I can get that close to. She knows a lot about me. In fact, she knows everything and she still says she loves me.

Susan's Current Friendships

Throughout her life, Susan has never had many long-lasting or close friendships. Partly this is a result of her frequent moves, and partly it is by choice. The idea of trusting someone is new. She traces the inability to trust back to the relationship she had with her parents.

S: I don't trust many people. I just have never been able to trust women. They lie a lot. You expect that from a man, but not from a female. My mom used to tell us kids things and I would believe her. When I grew up and found out that she had been telling us lies, it hurt me as much as when she would whip us with a broom handle. It was wrong for her to do that. I can't trust anyone. My daddy, he just totally wiped out my trusting a male. He done a job on me.

Her inability to trust, mixed with guilt over the events in her life, have made it difficult, if not impossible, for Susan to get close to people. She describes it as a "wall" between herself and the rest of the world. She has always been surrounded by men, but most of these relationships have been kept on a superficial level or have revolved around sex.

S: Most of the friends I have had on the streets were males. We would drive around, drink, and smoke dope. I never did go out with just females. As far as sexual deals, these friends weren't for that. Just to ride around and be buddies, just get high and get drunk with. If we would get so we couldn't walk, we would go someplace and pass out. When we woke up, we'd go again. I don't want that no more, but that is how I have lived.

The lack of communication with men extended into the marriages and common-law relationships Susan has had. She again describes a "wall" existing between herself and her partners—a fear of telling too much about her past for fear they would find a way to use it against her. When asked about the relationships with her past husbands and partners, she responded:

S: I have always just felt like a housewife. My duty was to take care of the kids, clean the house, and be there for him when he wanted to "get off."

During her stay in prison this time, Susan has met a woman who had similar experiences in her childhood. They have begun to forge a friendship based on sharing these common experiences. Susan is very excited about it, and yet confused because it appears to come with no strings attached.

S: I talk with her every day. She has had some of the same things happen to her as I have. I feel good when I talk to her. Me and her just sit around a lot and talk. She was beat by her parents, too, and I told her I could understand those feelings because I went through it. The other ones down here, they always want something from me, but she is different. The other day I offered her a cigarette, and she wouldn't take it. At first I got mad and said, "What is it, my cigarettes aren't good enough for you?" She said, "No, I just don't want nothing from you except to be friends. I don't want nothing you have." I said, "Well, all right then." Now I can't wait to meet her every afternoon and talk. I feel like I can tell her anything and it will be okay. I don't know why, but I do.

I: It sounds like it is nice to be able to share things and not have to worry if you will be accepted or end up being used.

S: Yeah, it is. I have never felt like that. I told her there are some things in my life that I am just now beginning to learn to talk about. I am not proud of them, but I am beginning to learn to talk about them and open up to other people. I told her I felt better now and one day I might want to share some of them with her. I told her if you keep it a secret, it will drive you crazy. I am ready to start feeling better about myself.

Being accepted by me and her new friend in the prison also seems to have allowed Susan to venture out and be more open to others. She is also coming to realize that the sexual relationship she had with her father may not be so unusual as she has thought all these years.

After one of our interview sessions, Susan returned to school. On my next visit, she related the following exchange that took place with a fellow classmate.

S: When I got back to the school the other day, this girl who sits next to me asked me where I had been. I told her I had been talking to a counselor. She kept asking me what we was talking about, so finally I said, "Have you ever heard of sex within the family?" She said, "Oh yes, I have slept with my uncle." I said, "How was it? Did he hurt you or make you do it?" She said, "Oh no, honey, my uncle is a hunk." I couldn't believe it. I think there is more of it going on, but no one is paying attention to it.

Susan seems to have no sense of what is appropriate and what is not appropriate in a friendship. It seems that because of her poor self-concept, Susan has always felt that she had to "buy" friendships, either with sex or material goods. She appears to slip easily into the role of mother for the other women in the prison and wants to give to them continually, often at her own expense. As the Christmas season approached, Susan had Mike send her a variety of art supplies. She tried to enlist the other women who lived in her quadrangle to join together and decorate for the holidays. She also had colored construction paper to make Christmas cards to send to people. None of the other women were interested. Susan was determined that they would all feel better if they had decorations and some holiday spirit, so she worked by herself and decorated the doors and windows on their quadrangle.

The theme of taking responsibility for everyone is one that occurs frequently in Susan's conversations. She worries about how Bill's mother will feel about the Christmas card she sent—that it may depress her more; she took the responsibility for the armed robbery so Bill would not be buried as a robber; she has Mike send money to the other women so they will not feel alone and do without; she frequently takes the blame for things that happen in the dormitory so that others will not be punished; and she frequently hides her own wishes, desires, and needs if she feels she will be responsible for making someone else feel badly.

While exploring this need to be responsible for others, we had the following exchange:

I: I wonder if sometimes your wanting to take the responsibility for everyone has anything to do with giving up your children for adoption and not being able to care for them?

S: Maybe . . . I guess so. I don't know where I went wrong, but I do know I probably could have done better by them. I have lots of regrets. I regret having my kids. I love them, but I regret having them. I hate my mother. I don't hate her as much as I used to. I hate her because she left this mark on me. She's the reason I gave up my kids. I just didn't know how to be a good mother.

I: So maybe by giving so much to others is the way you have learned to feel less guilty about giving your children up for adoption?

S: When I give, I feel good. Like I have really done something. But it don't look like I ever get back as much as I give. Do you reckon I have been trying to buy friendship? Like, people ask me for things all of the time, and I give it to them so they won't be without, or feel bad. I will go without instead. All I get is their attention for a short while.

In addition to the painful old memories, the talk of the holidays and the gathering of families has reminded Susan that she is indeed alone. It is something she previously said does not bother her. She has accused other inmates of being weak if they get depressed and miss their families or children.

S: Right now everyone is talking about their people all coming down here to the prison for Christmas. All I am saying is, "Well, I ain't got nobody." Then I go to my room and start thinking about it and realize that I really don't have nobody. I really am alone. . . .

It's just the point that I don't got nobody. It's never bothered me before. I have my boys' picture, but I don't even like to pull it out right now. The boys are the light of my heart. My little girls . . . I know this sounds terrible, but I never wanted girls to start with. My little boys are just . . . [silence].

I: Is the depression resulting from your not being able to see them?

S: And feeling guilty. Mostly feeling guilty because I think I could have done better. I was as bad a mother as my own was, and I never wanted to be like her. . . .

I am afraid to reach out and trust someone. I am afraid they won't understand how a mother could give her children away. . . .

I am afraid to get close to anyone. They always seem to throw it up in my face when they get mad at me or they leave. I want to tell people about me. I want them to care about me. I want to care about them. But, I am afraid. I want so much, I don't know, to be like everyone else I guess.

Susan's Future

Susan's immediate future will revolve around a transfer from the women's prison to a halfway house. To deter escapes, inmates are never advised before-hand when they will be transferred. The uncertainty of when the transfer will take place as well as the stress of being alone for the holiday season have taken their toll on Susan. She fears she will be provoked into a fight that will nullify her transfer. Also, she is not sure what will await her at the halfway house.

While she has been incarcerated, Susan has had all of her upper teeth pulled. She is very self-conscious about talking and smiling without her teeth. Because she is due to be transferred soon, and because there is a long waiting list for the dental clinic, there is a good chance that she will be transferred without her plates. Mike has told her not to worry, that he will not only pay for her to get plates, but also that he will pay the rent on an apartment and buy her a car.

Once she is transferred, Susan will be expected to get a job and to contribute to her support. Her previous work history has been sporadic. Because she lacks a high-school diploma and any vocational training, she cannot expect to secure a job earning more than minimum wage.

S: I will have to look for a job when I get to the halfway house. Whatever it is, though, I want it to be forty hours a week. I don't want one of these that is 18 hours here and 10 hours there. When I get tired of a job, I just start to lay out. And I don't want to be running from one to another. . . .

I have had a lot of different types of jobs in my life. I have worked as a maid, in a nursery with plants, at a photographer's studio as a receptionist, but mostly I have waitressed a lot. I think I can probably get a job as a waitress. The Waffle House and the Omelette Shoppe are always hiring.

I: Do you like being a waitress?

S: I don't know. I always seem to go back to that kind of work. I guess I like meeting the people. I would really like to go to cosmetology school, but I have to have a high-school diploma first. I would like to make something out of myself. I just want to be *something* . . . something so I don't have to depend on nobody else. I wish I could just put my past in a box and store it away. . . .

It's hard to change. I get tired, but I pray every night. I am doing better.

Susan will spend, barring any trouble, six months in the halfway house. After her release, her dream is to get an apartment with another woman who is currently in the women's prison with her. She says she wants to learn to take care of herself, learn to be independent, and possibly sometime in the future find a "nice man" and get married again. She is also planning on joining a therapy group for women who had a sexual relationship with a relative during childhood.

Until this point in her life, the fear of being alone often pushed Susan into loveless marriages and relationships. She feels she is just beginning to discover who she is and what she wants out of life. While this is very exciting, it is also very frightening. Given her history of drug and alcohol abuse and previous attempts at suicide, loneliness and death are never far from her thoughts.

S: I think I have always had a problem in that I am scared of being alone. I have always said I don't want to be alone.

I: I am not sure what you mean by "alone." I think there is a difference in being alone and being lonely.

S: Not having nobody. Like not being married. That scares me.

I: What is scary about it?

S: I don't know. I never thought about being able to take care of myself without a man. And going out to eat by myself or living by myself, forget it. And like sharing things when I get old. . . . When I had my kids, I used to think I just wanted to see them get grown and see my grandkids. That was my goal. But now, I am trying to find a purpose for living. A goal, you know?

I: Sounds like you had a whole picture of what was going to happen . . . the kids would grow up and have children of their own, and you would be involved in their lives. Now that that is not possible, it is hard for you to readjust or formulate new goals for your life?

S: Yeah, I know I should live for me, but that's hard. I get real tired. There are times when I talk to God and say, "Just please take me home."

Concluding our interviews, Susan was asked to project into the future and describe what she would see as being a "good" life for herself.

S: A good life for me would be to have somebody love me. No fussing, no fighting. A home . . . and not have to beg for it.

5
Judy's Life

J udy is a schoolteacher. She is Caucasian, five feet, five inches tall, and weighs 115 pounds. She has short brown hair and is always dressed in very feminine apparel. When she talks, her eyes seem to sparkle. She waves her hands in the air when she gets excited or to punctuate what she is saying. Her laughter is infectious. She appears much younger than her twenty-six years. At first glance, one might mistake her for a high-school cheerleader.

She is very open about the sexual relationship she had with her father, which lasted for twelve years—from the time she was five years old until she was a senior in high school and seventeen years old. Reaching the point of being comfortable talking about her experiences has not come quickly or easily. Judy was a battered wife in a disastrous first marriage; went through a period of promiscuity and drug abuse following her divorce; and has sought individual, group, and marital therapy in an attempt to come to grips with her past.

Judy's Childhood

Judy grew up in a middle-class family in a large southern city. She is the second of four children; the other three are males. Her father is a successful attorney who owns his own firm. Her mother has never worked outside the home. While the marriage has been rocky for many years, it was only within the past five years that Judy's parents divorced. The mother, still supported by the father, lives alone. Judy and two of her brothers live on their own, but her older brother lives with the father.

From outward appearances, the family seemed to be living the American Dream while Judy was growing up. However, inside the home were serious problems. Judy's mother is a diagnosed schizophrenic. She was frequently hospitalized during Judy's childhood and therefore was out of the home a large part of the time. Most of the daily responsibilities of running the home therefore fell on Judy.

There is a history of mental problems in Judy's mother's family.

J: My mom's father committed suicide. He was a manic-depressive. My mom herself is what they call a "burned-out schizophrenic" and my older brother has some problems. He lives with my dad now. They are both crazy. They get into big fights. My brother is twenty-seven now. He has never sought counseling or help, but he needs to. He is just living off dad and not making it on his own.

In addition to her mother's frequent hospitalizations, Judy believes her father's extramarital relationships weakened the marriage.

J: My dad had lots of women. He had a lot of affairs while he and my mom were married. After they got a divorce, he had a girlfriend about my age. He was in his late forties then. It just didn't work out. My dad can be real charming, though. He has never had any problems finding women. He can whip out fifty-dollar bills when he wants to. He can be real flashy. He has always had a lot of younger friends. That's how he got involved in drugs, he was being "cool." I really don't know why he kept having sex with me. I kept rejecting him in so many ways. I guess maybe I was a challenge. I mean he already had my mom and all of these girlfriends.

In retrospect, it seems impossible to Judy that the sexual relationship with her father lasted for twelve years, and no other member of the family indicated that they suspected anything. Her father initiated the sexual relationship when Judy was five years old. Over the twelve years, it escalated from inappropriate fondling and kissing, watching while Judy bathed or dressed, mutual masturbation, oral sex, and finally actual intercourse. As Judy sums it up, "My dad has been in every orifice I have."

All of the sexual activity took place in the home, usually at night with the other family members also in the house.

J: I feel like on some level my mom had to know. I remember there were times my dad and I would be in the bed with *her!* All three of us in the same bed! There were other times when she would walk into my room late at night and we were together in bed. Of course, when she came, everything stopped. She *never* said anything! Then there were other times when my dad would grab me in front of her and my brothers and French kiss me. Things like that . . . not letting me go, even with me struggling, holding me real tight. To me, that's real obvious!

One of her brothers recently related to her his perceptions of their growing-up years. Judy had called a family meeting of the mother and brothers to confront them with what she had gone through with the father.

J: One of my brothers told me he remembers my daddy destroying my credibility in the family and always saying ugly things about me. My brother said, "You were so good, you didn't cause any trouble, you didn't break things like the rest of us. You were the only girl, you were just good." He said he could never figure out why my dad would say the ugly things about me. But he also said if I had told him about the sexual relationship years ago, he would not have believed me because my dad had laid the groundwork to discredit me within the family. My dad is real persuasive. He is a real nut. To him, sex with me was not harmful to me.

Although nothing was said at the time, one brother evidently sensed that something about Judy's relationship to their father was not just "right."

J: When I was growing up I don't remember any of my brothers saying anything. I do remember that my oldest brother would always tease me and say things like, "How come you don't want to be next to Dad?" I thought he knew. I would get real mad and just stare at him. He is a year older than me. When I told him recently about the sex, he said he remembered saying those things and he was sorry. He said he didn't know anything was going on between me and dad, but I think he was picking up on something.

One thing that stands out in Judy's mind about her childhood years is that she tried to stay out of the house as much as possible. She says she was a great "joiner" and would become involved in any club or activity available. She also went to school early and stayed late in order to help teachers put up bulletin boards, clean up, or whatever, just so she would avoid being at home.

J: My brother said he knew I spent a lot of time in my room when we were teenagers. He says he doesn't really even remember seeing me much, which is true because I was gone. I was in every type of extra-curricular activity I could get in. I prided myself on being in this, this,

this, etc. I was real proud of that. And when I was home I stayed in my room. I would come out and help my mom cook sometimes, but I hated to do anything at home.

In order to stay out of the home, Judy had to find a supportive adult who was willing to transport her to the various activities. She found this in the mother of her best friend. She spent as much time with this friend and her family as possible, and Judy's father became very hostile about this relationship. Although he never forbid it, it was clear to Judy that he did not approve.

J: My best friend and I were *so* close. When she spent the night at our house we always slept in the same bed. One time my dad told me he thought we were lesbians. I didn't even know what the word meant. My friend did not like my dad. Most of the time she would invite me to spend the night at her house. I think my dad must have sensed that she didn't like him. I also think he resented us being so close all through school. One time he also told me he thought we were "conniving." We were just kids.

Although Judy became very close to this girl and her mother, she never told them about what was going on between her and her father.

J: Looking back, I think my dad may have been afraid that I would tell my friend what was happening between us. I almost did tell her. But I felt if I told her, she would tell her mother. They really loved me so I thought they would do something about it like call my dad or they would somehow confront him and then I would be in *big* trouble. Somehow I thought my mom would have another nervous breakdown and it would all be my fault. That the family would fall apart or something. I just didn't feel that there would be any good that would come out of telling.

Two particular incidents stand out in Judy's mind that illustrate the role confusion her dad felt for her. At the time of Judy's first communion, her mother was again hospitalized. She thinks this might be the first time she realized her dad related to her as an adult, rather than as a child.

J: I had a white dress and white veil for my first communion. My dad took me out to breakfast. I remember he took my arm and put it in his and told everyone in the restaurant, "She is my little bride." It was like I wasn't his little girl. I think I sensed something was weird about that. I remember being *real* uncomfortable.

A second incident occurred several years later, around Christmas.

J: He usually did not buy my mom gifts. I would remind him and finally it would end up that I would go out and get the gift and sign everyone's name to the card. But, he would give *me* things. One time he showed me this diamond ring and said, "I would like to give this to you. This really should be for you, but it is not the kind of gift a father would give his daughter so I am going to give it to your mother." He would just say things like that that indicated that I was special, but somewhere between a daughter, a wife, and a girlfriend.

The sexual relationship continued until Judy was a senior in high school. Her dad would either come into her room at night or enter the bathroom while she was bathing or getting dressed. She tried locking the door, but he would kick it in. She also tried pushing furniture in front of her bedroom door, but this only angered her father, and he came in anyway. When she was a senior in high school and going steady, she revealed the incest secret to her boyfriend.

J: I wanted to be a virgin. I was raised a Catholic and being a virgin when you married was real important. My parents always told me that I should save myself for my wedding night. To me it was important to be a virgin. But, I knew I wasn't one. Not that my boyfriend and I were planning on getting married or anything, but I think I felt I had to tell him so he would reject me and he would go out and find someone else. It was like I didn't feel good enough for him. When I told him about the relationship with my dad, he went right over to Sears and bought one of these locks with a key. He went into our house and put it on my bedroom door. I had a key to get into my bedroom. I gave my mother the other key in case there was a fire. My dad never said a word about the lock or about taking it off. I don't know if he ever tried to get in again or not. I locked it every night. It was real important to me that my boyfriend never told anyone and that he did not reject me. He asked me a lot of questions about what my dad did with me, but he was real understanding.

No one in the house ever openly acknowledged that the lock had been placed on Judy's bedroom door. Her father's almost nightly visits stopped, but she was still verbally harassed by him.

J: My dad would get real mad about the lock. Before it was on my door, I tried to put chairs or a dresser in front of the door because the original lock on the door was broken. It never worked. My dad would just kick it in and come in anyway. Once I had the lock my boyfriend put on there, my dad would say things like, "You think you have your own apartment don't you?" or "I don't know who you think you are." But, it ended his visits. I spent a lot of time in there by myself.

Judy's First Marriage

Judy's first marriage took place when she was twenty years old. She admits now that getting out of the house was a motivator for the marriage. She and John were both college students at the time. He was six years older than she and had returned to college after being in the army. He had a seven-year-old son from a previous marriage. The marriage lasted two years, and Judy recounts it as a tumultuous time in her life.

> J: I think the most stressful situation in my life has been my first marriage. I think the reason it was so stressful is that I was old enough to be aware of what was going on and seeing the same old patterns . . . like at one point I realized that I married someone like my dad and I had sworn up and down never to do that.

Shortly after their marriage, John became physically violent with Judy. She later learned that his physical violence had resulted in his first marriage ending in divorce. Judy asked John to seek counseling with her or by himself. He refused. He felt like he was getting "better," since Judy had not been hospitalized as his first wife had on several occasions.

> I: How would the fighting start?
>
> J: Sometimes he was drinking. But most of the time it was little things. Like maybe if I had cooked peas instead of carrots. Maybe he would throw something. He would say I couldn't cook and then I would tell him he could do the cooking then. But he always wanted me to cook so we had these arguments. He would throw something at me. I finally got to where I would fight back. I would throw it back at him. Then he might grab my arms and push me. I would push him back. If I fought back, oh brother, if I showed any rebellion, that was it. At the time, my hair was real long. He would just take my hair and hit my head against the wall or throw me on the floor and hit me just like I was a punching bag.

In addition to the physical violence, there were other problems in the marriage, mainly John's gambling and the drugs with which they both experimented. Also, since both of them were college students and only working part-time, money became a focal point of their disagreements.

J: I hated it when John would go out gambling. I felt like we couldn't afford it. We were mainly living off his VA money. He had been in the service before I met him. We were spending an awful lot on drugs. We spent more on drugs than we did on rent some months. It got to the point that that was enough! I would need shoes or a book. He hated it whenever I would disagree with him. I would complain and say things like, "How can you do that? We don't have the money." Then he would go out and shoplift and be real proud of it. Or we would go to a restaurant and he wouldn't pay the bill. We would get in the car and he would tell me he stiffed the waitress. I felt embarrassed. I never wanted to go back into certain restaurants.

The literature on battered women speculates that they often do not realize they are battered. They also frequently assume the blame for the battering. Judy was no different.

J: My dad had never physically abused me like that. And any other relationship I had had they had never done that either. I knew John had an explosive temper so I thought if I could just stop complaining so much about his gambling or the drugs . . . if *I* could do these things then everything would be better. . . .

I always blamed myself. He was always real nice afterwards, too. He would go out and spend money on me . . . buy me an album or some clothes, especially if he had torn up my clothes during a fight. He would be real nice for a few days. . . . He would say he was going to be better. Then I did not think of it as "battering" because the bruises would be on my head, but somehow they did not count because they did not show. They did not bleed. I minimized *a lot!* I assumed the responsibility for his behavior. But in the end I also had to assume the responsibility for doing something about it. If he was not going to counseling, then I decided I would go on my own. If I was the problem, then okay, let me get myself straight.

For a while, John was able to persuade Judy not to seek counseling. He would convince her that he really was doing better. He would remind her that she was not as severely beaten as his first wife. Compounding the situation was Judy's guilt and sense of shame. There was an unwillingness on her part to admit that she had made a mistake in marrying John.

J: John kept telling me that he was getting better and in some ways, I guess he was. Not as far as the actual beatings, though. But we would get into these brawls and he would go to my closet and rip up my clothes. I would be mad at him so I would break up his stereo. It was like we both were saying, "I am going to get you back!" It would eventually escalate into something physical. Or sometimes he would lock me out of the apartment. I would pound on the door until a neighbor would call the police. But, we did get to the point where we were not doing as much yelling and screaming, so maybe he was getting better.

In thinking back now, Judy finds it almost impossible to believe that she actually stayed in this relationship as long as she did.

J: When I think back about it, it is like it is not even me. We got to the point where we would fight but not tear up things. It was really embarrassing for people to come over to our apartment and see a lamp broken or whatever. I was so ashamed.

During this time, Judy also realized that she often blocked things or situations out of her consciousness if they were too painful. Another reason for her not leaving sooner was her beginning to question her own sense of reality.

J: One time we were fighting about something and I had on a new pair of shorts and shirt. John just ripped them off. He hurt his finger. Something happened to a tendon. He had to have an operation. At the time he was working where he had to lift things so he told people that he had hurt his finger at work. I started believing him myself, but I think I knew that it wasn't right. It was like I could picture the actual incident. I knew I blocked a lot. . . .

John got to where he blacked out a lot. His mother kept saying she thought he was a diabetic, but I don't know. One time he knocked me down and kicked me. I had a bruise on my hip. I couldn't roll over in bed; couldn't wear shorts. But then one day he saw it and asked, "What happened to you?" He did not seem to know that he did it. . . .

My brother knew what was going on with John and me, I think. My mom knew, my dad knew. I just wasn't ready to get out. My father told me that I should act like I was married . . . like it was *my* fault. I'll admit I had my part to play in it, but my dad was not protective at all.

Judy was working part-time to help make ends meet and taking college classes. She began to realize that she was "overloading" when she started "not thinking," but rather just going through the motion of daily activities.

J: I have a good memory, but I would forget where I left my keys. And I was not sleeping at night. Then I found I just started packing things. I had a shoe box that I put all of my make-up in. Anything that was mine I started putting into boxes. I was doing things like getting all of my clothes in certain drawers. I know now I was preparing to leave, but at the time I couldn't admit it. John thought I was spring cleaning.

Judy realized she was not performing at her job. She confided in her supervisor. She still had not consciously admitted to herself or to anyone else that she planned to leave the marriage.

J: When I left I really had not intended to leave. John kept telling me he wasn't going to counseling. But I knew I had to. I could not function any more I was so keyed up . . . not at home, at work, in school, any place. . . .

When I did start talking to my supervisor she said I was "too capable" to be ruining my life. I told her John and I were having problems and having violent fights and that he was beating me. She called a battered women's shelter. I talked with them, but they were forty miles away. I didn't think I could go there. They told my supervisor, which was the best thing that ever happened to me, "If she wants help, she can call us." I didn't even know at the time that I was a "battered" woman. I had bruises, but they didn't show. My nose wasn't broken and I didn't have any black eyes. But, a day later I called the shelter and asked for a "definition" of a battered woman. I was being very intellectual. The lady told me, "Anything from one slap to a severe beating." That was it. I said, "Oh no, I might be one."

The idea of admitting that she was a battered wife scared Judy into action. She sought out some women at work to talk to and found she was denying the seriousness of the problem.

J: When I told them at work what was going on at home, they told me I was stupid to stay. They didn't say, or at least I didn't hear them say, "Judy, you are worth so much more than that." What I heard was, "You are so stupid." So I just shut up. I tried to hold everything in all by myself. Every time I would pass the battered women's shelter when I rode the bus, I found myself looking, staring in fact, in hopes of seeing someone who was really bruised.

One final fight with John convinced Judy that she could not stay in the marriage as it was. The violence had reached such a pitch that she not only thought of killing John, but also of taking her own life.

J: It was scary to admit that I was battered. It's like what I imagine it is like for an alcoholic to get up in front of a group and say, "I am an alcoholic." I was never like I was with John before we married. I did not grow up with an explosive temper. But at one point I realized that I had the potential to kill him . . . that it was in me to kill him and me. I prayed, "Oh God, please don't have me go to jail for killing him." To me that would be the worst, to be put in jail. But one time he locked me out of the apartment with just my T-shirt and underwear on. I banged on the window until it broke and I cut my arm. I went into the kitchen and got a knife and decided to kill him. I had just had enough! Then I wondered if it would be worth it. He would be dead and not feel anything and I would be in jail. So I decided "No, this is not worth it, I'll just kill myself." I started to and something . . . there's always hope in this life, so I put the knife down.

Although she was afraid and embarrassed, Judy called the battered women's shelter again.

J: I was afraid they would say, "Oh you are just a little wimp," but they didn't. They said, "Yes, you have a problem." So I made an appointment and once I make an appointment, I keep it. So the next day I had no money to go down to the shelter on the bus. I couldn't ask John for the money so I told a friend what I was going to do. She gave me bus money and ten extra dollars. It was a really strange day. Right before John left for school, we made love. We had been having terrible fights. I pretended that I was going to class, too, but I went to the bus station. When I got to the shelter and talked with them, I realized that I was a battered woman. I asked them what they thought the chances of me working my marriage out were. They said, "Zero. If he doesn't see this as a problem, it is zero." When they told me zero, it really seemed realistic. I called John and told him where I was. He was real mad. I told him I needed help, and I wanted him to help me get this help. He said, "Just don't come back." Having to make the decision to leave him was hard. It came down to *I* had to do something about it. At that point I had had it, and I said, "Okay, I am not coming back." For about two months before this I had been telling him, "John, when I leave I am leaving for good. I am not going to play games . . . leave, come back; leave, come back. When I leave that will be it." He didn't take me seriously. I didn't go back.

After she went to a friend's house to stay, Judy tried to talk with John's mother about his problems. The mother was already aware of John's beating his wives, but refused to think of it as a serious problem. She was of no support to Judy.

J: I called his mother and told her that I had been to the shelter and that I wasn't going back to John. She acted like it was *my* fault. Like it was my fault that I had left to get help. She was really upset, but not because of what he and I were doing to each other, but because, as she put it, "Well, now I can't go to Mississippi this weekend and it is your fault." I told her I was sorry that I ruined her trip, but I wasn't going back. His family wanted me to go back to him because he needed "help," my help. I was tired. I felt like I was the one who needed help. . . . They also felt he was getting better because he did not beat me as bad as his first wife. I mean he broke her teeth and her bones. She had to be hospitalized. So they thought he was getting better, and maybe he was. But I don't care if you are breaking bones or just slapping someone around every week, it is just not cutting the mustard.

Judy stayed with a girlfriend. This friend volunteered to go get all of Judy's belongings from the apartment. Judy was surprised, but pleased that she had organized and packed everything so the friend could just go by and collect it.

J: I just whipped out a list of where the boxes were. I told her, "You don't have to go through anything, just go get the boxes." It was just boom, boom, boom. Then she told me she was afraid that John might shoot her so I just said, "forget it." By then John had thrown out most of my things. But, my dad said he would give him $200 if he would bring the things left to our house. He did bring a few things over.

Since her divorce, Judy has read and studied about battered women. At one point she was even talking about her experiences in front of groups in hopes of helping someone else get out of such a marriage or situation.

J: After I started reading some things on battered women, I realized that John was an accomplished beater. He did not put any knocks on my body that were noticeable for a long time. This is a sign of an experienced batterer. I had bruises on my back and stuff, but no one could see them. When I read that, it really frightened me. I don't know what would have happened if I hadn't left.

Judy's Move to Another State

Soon after she left John, Judy realized that she could not stay with her family and receive any support. She also knew that if she stayed in the area, she would eventually weaken and go back to John. Therefore, she quickly made up her mind to move to another state.

J: After three or four days, I called a cousin in another state. I didn't even know her very well. I just packed up and went to live with them for about three months. My aunt kept telling me, "Just relax. Don't worry, just relax." But I knew I needed to get a job real soon. I knew if I didn't put my roots down quick I would go back. I was so afraid. By the second week, I had a job.

After she got the job, Judy enrolled in a university to complete her under-graduate degree. She also located a female roommate. She describes her first apartment as being furnished with Goodwill specialties. But, at least she had the feeling it was home. And, it was hers.

J: I knew I was kinda wishy-washy. I had to do something. I was *going* to get my degree, and I was *going* to make something of my life. *Nobody* was going to stop me. I think that idea got entangled in my marriage to John somehow because I was so afraid that he would take a career away from me; that he would get me pregnant and mess everything up! I did not want to be a dime-store clerk with three or four kids at home. I had a vision for myself. He was getting in the way . . . I knew what I could do with my life if I could just get the gar-bage cleared out.

I: Where did the vision/dream come from?

J: When I was a teen-ager I had some horrible times. I was real, real depressed. I felt like if a Mack truck could just roll over me . . . but I never did anything along those lines. It was just a thought, but I think it was suicidal. I got real low. Somewhere along the line I started lis-tening to my teachers. When they talked generally in class and said things like, "If you want to change, you *can change*. You can do *any-thing* that you want to." I believed it. They were not talking specific-ally to me, but I believed them.

Her parents' families of origin also had some influence. Although it was her father's side of the family that inspired her to greater goals, it is her mother's side that she still keeps in touch with. She feels they are more down-to-earth. Her father's family is socially and economically better off than her mother's family.

J: On my mother's side of the family, they seemed to have this attitude like, "Well, this is just the way it is." I kept thinking, "No, it can't be like this. Look at other people, they don't live like this." But it was almost as if they were destined to a certain way of life. I just couldn't see it like that. I was just very aware that there were so many opportu-nities. . . .

Part of it comes from my father's side of the family, I guess. They were well-off. They all went to college and are doctors and lawyers. They had done something with their lives. It was hard for my mother's family. They did the best they could, I guess, but I just couldn't settle for it. I knew I would do whatever I had to to make *something* of my life, too.

Judy's Therapy

Once she had relocated in another state, Judy became active in a local church. Although raised a Catholic, she found she was more comfortable in another denomination. She is a born-again Christian. Her relationship with the church has offered her strength and solace. Her social life began to revolve around activities at the church. It was during this time that she became best friends with Lynn. Over a period of time, Lynn confided in Judy that she had been sexually abused by her father. She had been in therapy for many years and as a result was able and willing to discuss her abusive experiences openly. Lynn's openness allowed Judy to reopen some painful memories from her own past.

> J: I had *never* talked to anyone about the sex with dad so freely until Lynn came along. She was the first person I knew who had had the same experience. In the beginning, I tried to tell her that I didn't have a problem with it. She talked me into going to the psychology department of the university to be a subject in a study they were doing on incest. I went just to prove to Lynn that I didn't have a problem. You know, "I am a rock" and all of that. I felt like I was going to blow the interviewer away, but then when I left I realized that I had no inflection in my voice. I was so aware that I didn't feel *anything*. I knew then that I had a problem. I started to talk more about it and then Lynn and I found out about a group therapy program for women who had had similar incest experiences. We went to the group. It was horrifying. It was like I couldn't believe what they were saying. I started remembering all that stuff in my childhood and I couldn't believe that I had actually gone through that time. I had blocked all of it out of my consciousness.

Judy and Lynn eventually came to realize that they did not fit in with this group of women. Several of the women were lesbians and were very angry at all men. A couple of others were prostitutes. And yet, they had found comfort in the idea of a group of women who had had an incestuous experience in their childhoods. So, Lynn and Judy located a male and a female therapist who were willing to begin an incest-survivor group. For several years, both of them attended the weekly sessions of this group.

J: Talking to the interviewer at the university opened up a whole can of worms, but I am glad that I did it. In the first group I went to, I let them know, "I am not a lesbian or a prostitute. I'm kinda in between and I am doing pretty well." But then, the memories started coming back. I started *trying* to remember and writing all of this stuff down, then the feelings came back . . . the horror of it all! The real horror to me was that the sex with my dad had lasted for so long and no one knew about it, and if they did, nobody said anything. And it went on for twelve years! Maybe a one-shot thing you can get over, but a consistent twelve-year thing is a *big* part of your life. The shock to me was that at the time, I did not grieve. I didn't say or feel anything.

Once Judy began getting "in touch" with the blocked material, she not only attended the weekly therapy group meetings, but also started individual therapy. The realization that she had actually blocked a twelve-year segment of her life from her consciousness frightened her.

J: I don't ever want to be that defensive about anything any more. You know, where my mind has to protect me without my giving it permission to. I don't want twelve-year lapses to go on for the rest of my life. Back then, I didn't know what "resources" and "support systems" were. I tried to handle it on my own and couldn't deal with it, so I blocked it out. After all, I was only a kid. But I think dealing with the experience as an adult was more painful than the actual sex I had with my dad. I think it is easier to block it when it is going on than to go back and remember. You see it so differently as an adult. It's hard to go back and relive what happened. I was shocked. I found that I was having anxiety reactions, things I never experienced when I was a child and in the middle of it.

One result of Judy's individual and group therapy experiences was a desire to return to her family and reveal to them the incest secret she had harbored alone for so many years. About two years ago, she made the trip home for the express purpose of telling her mother and her three brothers what had taken place sexually between herself and the father during those twelve years.

J: When I told my family is when I really started dealing with it. I really wanted them to be supportive and loving. I was really in *need* at that time for their love and support. I wanted someone to say, "I am sorry that you went through that," or "Judy, we love you." I *needed* that from *them*. I noticed that my brothers did not stay in the same room with me alone for the rest of the weekend once they knew. One of them even got real angry with me. He said, "Why are you bringing this up now?" But, the other two brothers were real supportive, or as much as they could be. They knew I was telling the truth, but I guess they couldn't deal with it . . . it was just too heavy. And that *hurt* . . . it was like, "Now I have to go through this alone, too?" But I really did not have to go through it alone this time because I had the women in the therapy group, a whole new life, and new friends who were supportive. I really can't expect to go back and expect my family to give me what I didn't get in the first place.

During this trip home, Judy also planned a confrontation with her father. She says she wanted to talk to him as one adult to another, and she really only wanted him to acknowledge what had taken place and to say he took the responsibility for the sexual relationship ever happening. To this date, he has been unable to do so. In place of assuming the responsibility, he made remarks such as, "I can't believe you are bringing this up now, you were only a child and you should have forgotten that by now," or, "It didn't hurt you." Judy says there are many questions today that she would like to be able to discuss with her father in hopes of resolving some remaining problems and issues in her life. These questions include, "Why did you do it?"; "Have you felt the least bit guilty all of these years?"; or "Are you sorry?"

At this point, Judy has given up hope that her father will ever be able to face the situation and assume his responsibility for it occurring.

J: I would really like to talk to him now that the anger is not so strong on my part. I feel like now I would really like to have a conversation with him and try to find out what he was thinking back then. Like what he thought about that lock and key on my bedroom door? We have never really talked about the actual incest, and now since he has been experimenting with drugs, I am not sure that his mind is intact enough to do so.

Judy's concern for her father's mental state grew out of his arrest last year for possession and intent to sell drugs. After his arrest and before his trial, Judy says he frequently called her making veiled threats of suicide. Often his conversations made no sense at all.

While Judy is not clear about the circumstances, her father was acquitted of the charges. She said when she learned of the verdict through her mother she felt a real sense of anger and sorrow. Unconsciously, she had been hoping he would be convicted so she could then say to people who thought of her father as a bright, successful attorney, "See, I am not crazy. It wasn't me!"

Judy's Second Marriage

Judy went through a sexually promiscuous period before she became a born-again Christian and met and married her second husband, Jack. They had been married for two and half years when these interviews took place. Jack is also a schoolteacher and had been in a previous marriage that ended in divorce.

> J: I think probably five years ago, I wouldn't have picked Jack to marry. I don't think I was far enough along then. He was maybe "too good" for me, or maybe not emotional enough; or maybe just not crazy enough. He is very "even" and very supportive. I think I used to be addicted to feelings . . . my feelings. If things were going really good, I didn't trust that. I was afraid, worried that it was not going to last. Then when something did happen, I was sure that I had a part in having everything explode. If things weren't either real high or real low, I didn't know how to act.

Jack's quiet, easy manner and even demeanor is a theme that crops up frequently when Judy discusses their marriage.

> J: Jack is so supportive. He does not hold any law on me. He doesn't say, "You have to do this," or "You are stupid if you don't do that." He just says, "Do whatever you want to do," or "You are a big girl now, you can make your own decisions," and then I catch myself saying, "Oh yeah, I am." But he has added that, confirmed that feeling in me. So now, I don't doubt myself as much. I don't doubt my feelings. I accept my feelings and that has made my life a whole lot better. Before I met Jack, I always said I just wanted to be "even." I think I always looked for it, I just didn't know how to find it. Finally, I realized, "Oh yeah, Jack adds to that feeling."

Judy attributes part of the strength of their marriage to the fact that they genuinely like each other. She likes the feeling of being friends and not needing to compete with each other. Also, she finds an honesty and openness that was missing from her first marriage.

> J: I don't want to have to learn ways to "cope" any more. I don't want to have to figure out ways to "survive" any more. I want to deal with what is going on in the here and now. I am really learning to relax now with Jack because I don't feel I always have to be "one step ahead." He loves me and does not think I am a "wimp." He is real accepting. During the first part of our marriage a lot of things came back from the

marriage with John, like my cooking. I had questions constantly
about, "Was I good enough?" So now Jack says things like, "Oh, I *like*
scorched pudding," or "Don't worry, I *like* burnt toast." We laugh
about the things that John and I used to fight about. Jack knows that I
need room to grow. I am more willing, more confident to try new
things now. It carries over to all parts of my life. Even in my job,
which is very stressful. I have decided the object of the game is not to
add stress, but it is to take it off. I am going through life getting the
stress, the extra stress, off. I feel more now. I used to be comfortable
when I was overloaded and could say, "Hey, look at me, I am really
overloaded and I can do it." Now that the stress is manageable, I am
paranoid. Sometimes, I still have to wait a minute and say, "Wait a
minute, this is how it is supposed to be."

Judy's Career

Judy teaches special education, a job she finds stressful and demanding. She is
finding she is able to set limits for herself without bowing her head in shame
because she is not "Superwoman." Knowing what those limits are, and being
able to be assertive about them has been very helpful for her. She recently had
a discussion concerning the overenrollment in her classes and took her concerns to her male principal and also to the male county superintendent. While
she feels she was very assertive in stating her position, she came away with
feelings she identified as being similar to those she had in the incestuous relationship. For example, the two male "authority" figures told her to, "Be
quiet."; "Keep this a secret."; "Don't cause trouble, we'll take care of this."

> J: At work I am becoming more open and honest, too. I think I am
> beginning to be more direct with people. I used to think, "Oh no, I
> can't say that," but now I just tell people what is on my mind. It's like,
> before I didn't think I was worthy, now I feel better about myself.

While she is teaching, an area of particular concern to Judy is the identification of elementary-school children who are in abusive situations. On more
than one occasion, once a child has been identified as being sexually abused,
Judy has marched into the principal's office and *demanded* that appropriate
action be taken. She has caused more than a few eyebrows to be raised, especially when one principal asked her what her interest was in the matter, and
she revealed her own incestuous experience.

> J: Now I am not afraid to speak up. Before, I would never have openly
> talked about my experiences, but now I feel if the other person can't

deal with it, that's their problem. Also, with the children, it has helped me when I have had a "feeling" that one of them was being sexually abused to have someone confirm my hunch. I keep wanting to tell myself, "I am not crazy." And sometimes I even say that to folks and they say, "I know you are not crazy." But it is like I am always trying to convince myself that I wasn't crazy growing up. I knew what was going on. But it was like a little kid screaming for help and no one hears you.

Judy had the disadvantage of growing up without an adult available to serve as a "reality check." She says that only recently has she been able to stop doubting herself and her feelings.

J: Growing up, I had to go on nonverbal clues to survive. When I saw a certain look in my dad's eyes, I knew. I knew what was going to happen. I thought, "Oh no, here we go again." I was only five years old at the time, but I *knew*. But, I didn't trust my feelings enough. I kept thinking, "Oh well, maybe he won't." I didn't believe them enough to say, "Mama, no! I don't want to go to bed early tonight," because that was when he would come to my room. I guess I just never learned to trust my feelings.

Another instance in which Judy had negative feelings that she was unable to attend to occurred prior to her first marriage. She says now that these feelings were more than just "bridal jitters."

J: Right before our wedding, I knew it was wrong. I had so much proof, but I just didn't or couldn't say "no." I tried to, but then I changed my mind because I thought, "Next week you will be in love with him again." I just didn't trust my feelings at all.

In addition to the individual, marital, and group therapy Judy has been involved with, she attributes a large part of her learning to trust her feelings to extensive reading and talks with friends.

J: Reading probably has helped me the most. Mostly I read about battered women and incest. Just even the little bit I have read helped me to say, "Yeah, I was right." I think that counseling has helped, too. It kinda brought everything into focus for me. I mean, even though my perceptions may be wrong and I still have to take into consideration, a lot of them are more right than wrong.

Not doubting herself and being able to trust her feelings have enabled Judy to examine her career goals. She is currently working on a master's degree in special education. She is also in the process of starting to sell cosmetics in direct sales. Jack supports her in these new ventures. He said that if she wants to sell cosmetics full time next year, and not return to teaching, that would be okay with him. It has been very important to Judy to have Jack's support in this matter.

> J: I don't doubt myself as much as I used to. I think it is because I have started to realize that if I surround myself with people who are supportive and seek those people out, it helps me not to be as doubtful. I think that's the main thing, I don't doubt myself as much as I used to.

This new found self-confidence and openness has allowed Judy to meet and make a host of new friends. It has been helpful for Judy to learn what it is they like and admire about her.

> J: I think men admire me because they tell me that I am real easy to be around. That always thrills me for someone to say that. Men also say that I don't make them feel like they have to act in a certain way, make a lot of money, or have a certain type of car, etc. That I wasn't really expecting something from them. They could be themselves. Finally, that I am real easy to talk to, which is a real compliment since for so much of my life I didn't really *talk* to anyone. I think I do have a tendency to create an atmosphere. It's like I open the door and let them come in to tell me all of their "stuff." Then I weigh it to see how much I want to tell them about me. I need to know where they are coming from. Also, some have said they admire my sense of humor. . . .
>
> I haven't had as much feedback from women, but recently one woman did tell me, and it really thrilled me, "You know what I really like about you is your sense of humor. You can laugh at a lot of problems." I never realized anyone had noticed that before. Also, another friend wrote recently and told me she admired my loyalty . . . being there when she needs me. . . .
>
> Another thing that I admire in other people but I hadn't really thought they admired about me is my faith. Everyone has a different view of God. When I started seeing so much strength in myself . . . like God didn't really want me to be a whimpering little idiot. He has given me so much victory and power! I had to stop weaseling around. It's just part of me now and some people admire that.

In concluding the interviews, Judy was asked, "What would be a 'good life' for you?"

J: Not too many worry problems . . . mainly money problems. Not too many ups and downs emotionally. I think being able to trust people and being able to better know who I am. My life is 100 percent better than it used to be.

6
Nancy's Life

At twenty-eight years old, Nancy has a long-desired career in advertising, a loving husband, and a healthy nine-month-old daughter, Monica. Nancy is an attractive, five-foot, two-inch, 105-pound, Caucasian brunette with plentiful energy and an infectious laugh. She frequently gets up and moves around while she talks. Her interest in jogging and tennis are reflected in her flexibility and easy movement.

Her initial sexual contact with an adult occurred with a middle-aged farm hand on her father's farm. A year later she had a similar experience at the hands of her father. She was five and six years old at these times. Only in the last three or four years has Nancy been able to verbalize these experiences. Although many questions remain in her mind about them, she does not consider the sexual encounters with her father detrimental in her life.

Nancy's Childhood

Nancy is the third oldest of six children. She has two older brothers—33 and 30. She is 28 and has a brother who is 22, a sister 21, and a brother 20. During her childhood, her father owned six farms and was not only a successful farmer, but also an elected school superintendent for three terms. Her father was considered a pillar of the community.

> N: People who knew me when I was growing up thought that I came from a perfect home . . . Ozzie and Harriet. Every summer my dad would have about ten guys come live on our farm. It was basically to teach them responsibility. They were in total control of their own time, what they did, everything. The only rule was that they had to be at his breakfast table with him at 6 A.M. He didn't care if they came in from the night before at 6 A.M. He was willing to help people that way, not just his family. I guess if I had gone up to him and

said I wanted to talk, he would have been very open. I just never have felt comfortable doing that with him.

Nancy's family has lived in the same small southern town for three generations. Her father grew up in a poor family. He was the only son in a family of ten children, and he was the only one who graduated from college. He worked his way through school and is only five or ten credit hours away from a doctorate. After a tour of service in the Navy during World War II, he returned to his hometown. At the time of his return, Nancy's mother was one of her father's sister's best friends. Nancy describes their courtship and marriage as follows:

N: My dad was very, very handsome . . . deep dark hair with those bedroom eyes. He's very distinguished-looking today. I mean, if you saw my dad right now you would think he's a nice-looking, older man. I don't think they [the parents] ever really *loved* each other. My dad was a deacon in the church, and he has always been real religious. He was a Sunday school teacher until these last couple of years. My mom is also very religious, and she wanted to marry someone who was religious and who could provide for the family. Someone who was ambitious and who could provide well for her and their children. . . .

My dad married her on the rebound. He told me one time when he was drunk that he had been crushed by this other woman. He had gone off to World War II, and when he came back, she had married someone else. I think he married my mom just to show this other woman, I don't think he ever really has loved my mom. I don't think they even know what *real* love is.

The lack of affection between the parents carried over into their relationships with their children. Nancy regrets not having the freedom as a child to sit down and talk with her parents, but also feels she never learned as a child how to express her feelings.

N: Dad never gave us affection. To my mom either. You never saw them hug and kiss. My dad would cut up with her sometimes, come in and kiss her on the neck, but it always seemed so fake. My father felt that he was showing us his love by giving us all the material things we ever wanted.

Combined with the lack of emotion and affection, strict discipline was expected and enforced by her father. He was the patriarch, the utmost authority. Nancy thinks all this helped contribute to the facade of the "perfect" family.

> N: I came from a very, very strict family. When we sat down to dinner, we ate. We did not cut up and play. Out of six children I would say that none of us ever got to be a "normal" kid. When I went to a friend's house to spend the night and the parents brought me home, they would always tell my mom, "Nancy is such a little lady. I can't get over how good she is."

Not being able to feel close to either parent, Nancy developed her first close relationship with an adult with her fifth-grade teacher. This woman stands out as a pleasant memory of elementary school, although their relationship was short-lived.

> N: She was like an adoptive mother. I could talk to her and would have done anything in the world for her. Up until I had her for a teacher, I almost failed in school. My parents really should have kept me back, but that was beneath my father's dignity, as he was the school superintendent. Never since I was in the first grade had I made the honor roll until I had this teacher. I made the honor roll all the way until Christmas, when she left to have a baby. The teacher who replaced her and I did not get along. I hated her. I almost failed about three classes that year. But I think it bothers me more now than then because my parents just never got on me about grades. My parents never sat down and worked with me on school work. I was actually jealous of my friends who would come in and say they were put on restriction because of their grades. My parents never put me on restriction because of grades. . . .
>
> I have found out I am slight dyslexic. I didn't know until about two years ago when I was reading a magazine article and the title said, "If you can read this headline you are slight dyslexic." Mine is not real bad, but when I read that article, I realized what had been going on. I always transposed or reversed letters. The teachers and my parents thought I just couldn't read or spell. All the teachers ever said to my parents was that I just wasn't trying, and my parents accepted that. I was really mad at my parents because they did not try to find out what my trouble was.

Another vivid memory of her childhood is the theme, "You don't make waves." Nancy took on an adult role early in her life so as not to cause any trouble.

N: It seems I have always felt that I had to keep everything under control. I didn't cause waves. I mean, at home it was always, "Don't upset anyone." That has probably hurt me the most, and I still have that problem. I will keep things inside of me when I really want to chew somebody up one side and down the other.

One way to avoid making waves at home was to become involved in many school activities so that she was not at home any more than was absolutely necessary.

N: I was into every extracurricular activity there was. I am not good at sports, but I played them all. One thing I hate about my parents is that they were so strict. I could have probably done a lot more and been a lot more creative, but my parents frowned on extracurricular activities because they were not of any "real" substance. I played basketball for four years, and my parents *never* came to see one game. Another example is that I took piano lessons and really enjoyed playing. The teacher was such a witch! I figured out later that she was probably an alcoholic. She used to hit my hand with a ruler if I made a mistake. I wanted to keep taking so bad that I never told my parents. If I took from anyone else, they would have had to take [drive] me, and I didn't want to inconvenience them. Also, I was afraid if I told them, my dad would just tell me to stop taking altogether. Or, being the school superintendent, he would fire her. . . .

In high school, I hated home. I hated to go home. I would walk into the house and go straight to my room and not come out until the next morning. My parents would come back to my room and say, "Don't you want to come eat?" I would just tell them I wasn't hungry. I would just sit alone and listen to albums. I hated the town we lived in. I hated my family. I hated the whole thing. All I did was pretend to get out of that town and have the life I wanted . . . I came from the all-American family, had the all-American dad, a loving mom, the whole thing. . . .

When my dad was the school superintendent and successful in farming, we had anything we wanted materially. On the surface, everything looked and was *great!* For the longest time I lived that kind of lie. I wanted everyone to believe that we did have the all-American family. It was tough for me to admit that I came from very much less than the perfect family. When it really used to break my heart was when things that were big for me were not big for them. Like my basketball games, or one time when I ran for class president and didn't get it. I mean, did I get an "It's okay?" . . . nothing. I really never had anyone to talk to. I think my parents were just ignorant about raising kids. They had no idea how to parent . . . if it wasn't like they were raised, forget it. They had six kids, and we have all turned out just great. . . . That's amazing to me.

With two older brothers, Nancy easily fell into the roll of tomboy. She says she has always had more male friends than female friends and has enjoyed the competition with males more.

N: I have always found it hard to play silly little girl roles. That is one of the reasons I have never felt like I fit in. I always thought it was because of what had happened [sexually] to me when I was a little girl—that maybe that was why I was like that. Now I think it was just the way my parents raised me. I never knew how to let my true feelings out because I was afraid people would think I was "weird." My parents never talked to me. I just kept thinking I was weird because of the things that had happened. I felt that I was different.

As the three younger children were born, Nancy took on more and more of the mother's role in the family. She thinks of her mother as being very "weak" and unable to be a good mother.

N: All of her kids always have taken care of her, protected my mother. It's like my mother is really very self-centered and doesn't even know it. She only thinks of herself, but she doesn't think she does. I would love to hear from her on my birthday, but she doesn't think about that. But, come her birthday. . . . Also, what is really weird is that for someone who supposedly dedicated her life to her children and her husband, she doesn't do all that stuff of mothering. She never has. She is really very lazy. She believed that once I got old enough, I was supposed to clean the house, help her out. I ended up doing the whole thing. . . .

I was very bitter that my brothers did not have to do jackshit around the house. It was really like we were two families because of the age differences. After my older brothers had gone from home, I took care of the younger ones. If they wanted to tattle, they would come tattle to me. I would be the one who sometimes punished them or said, "Okay, you do this or that." All of my life I have had to take on a lot of adult roles. . . .

There's a lot of anger toward my parents. It's almost turned to pity now, though. For the longest time, I was angry because they were not the parents that I wanted them to be. They are neat people, but as parents, they stink. . . .

My father was a chauvinistic pig. He still is. We would get into yelling, screaming fights. I wish I had a dime for every time he kicked me out of the house. I used to plan things. Like I would be awful to my mother, ignore her, not tell her where I was going . . . not to hurt her, but to set up a fight with my father. I would set it up so I would say just the right thing and set him off so I could pop back exactly like I planned. He would say something like, "I demand that you show your mother more respect." I would look him right in the eye and say, "Why should I, you don't."

Once Nancy graduated from high school and began college in another town, the difference in how she perceived herself and how others perceived her was magnified.

N: When I was in high school, but mostly in college, a lot of girls were jealous of me. Even though I didn't realize it or view myself that way, I am not bad looking. I would always have a date, and I could go out with anyone I wanted. A lot of girls were jealous, and they would say things like, "Look at Nancy. She just thinks she is hot shit." Here I was thinking, "This poor little deprived person." When I was voted the Little Sister in the fraternity, that is when it brought out the jealousy in some people.

While Nancy was away at college, struggling with these personal issues, her family was struggling with their own problems. The family fortunes were plummeting.

N: When I left for college, everything started to cave in. My father became an alcoholic. He lost his ass. Partly because of the economy and partly because he pissed away the money. He went from having six farms with a total of about 6,000 acres, to nothing. The only way my mother could have any control was to have him legally removed from the premises and put a summons on his head that said if he stepped on the property, he would go to jail. After thirty-eight years of marriage, they went through a divorce.

I: After listening to you talk about your mother, I wonder where she got the strength to divorce your dad?

N: Part of it was me. When I became of an age to sit down and talk to my mother as an adult, I asked her, "Why do you take his shit?" I told her, "There's a whole big world out there that you can survive in without that asshole." She had never thought like that. She is real religious. I told her that if God was so wonderful and good, he didn't put us on this earth to live through hell. I kept telling her the God I believe in did not put me here to be unhappy. He is also not going to just go "Shazaam" and everything will be great and wonderful, but he will give you the strength to get what you want. Still, it took me years of saying that and his getting worse and worse and threatening to do physical harm, although I don't think he would. But, the man is psychotic. He loses his temper very quickly and can go into an absolute rage. The only time I ever know he hurt anybody was my brother. My father jumped on him one time and flew into a rage. He picked up a stick and hit him on the back. To this day it upsets my father because he really believes that this is the reason why my brother has back problems. The doctors have said that it is because he has an extra vertebra, but my father still blames himself. It was a lot easier for the kids in the family who were strong-willed to get along with my father. The ones who were more like my mom, they were just mush. They were shit in my father's eyes.

While talking to her about the possibility of divorce, Nancy considered telling her mother about the sexual molestation she had experienced by her father, but decided against it. However, she knew that such information would give her mother the leverage she would need in a divorce action.

N: My mom was petrified to divorce my dad because he had told her he wasn't going to give her a thing. I told her, "Mother, take my word, you can have anything that bastard has, and I have the key to all of it. You can take him for everything he's got. Just make a list of what you want. "She asked me, "Nancy, how?" I told her not to ask, but she could tell him I told her so. My father never said anything about it.

Her parents were eventually divorced, but have since remarried each other. A man whom her father had befriended years previously offered him a consulting job, which he took for several years. Once her father retired from this work, the benefactor then offered him some land, if he would make the payments on the property.

N: My mom and dad live in a small town, up on a lake, in a gorgeous house with a great view. They live there by themselves, and it is the best thing that ever happened to them. Because they are not around anyone they have to impress. They fight like cats and dogs, and it's great because they have never done that before. His word was always the gospel. Now she will nag the hell out of him. Even though my dad would like for people to think that the only reason he went back to my mother is that they are both getting old and don't want to live alone, it's bullshit.

Nancy's Sexual Relationship with Her Father

N: It wasn't until about three years ago that I said out loud that my father had fondled me. Then I started realizing a lot of things about myself that I had blocked out. I found out a lot of things I had done in my life, I did so I could push them down his throat. In reality, I don't think it made a shit to him.

Once she was able to admit out loud that she had been molested as a child, Nancy was able to put other things in her life in a different perspective also. She reviewed and examined the sexual atmosphere in her childhood home and came to realize that she has fewer long-term effects than people might expect.

N: I have come to realize that there are a lot of people who are sick when it comes to sexual activities, a lot more sick than me. I think when you first start feeling sexual, you feel guilty because you enjoy it. You don't think you are supposed to, at least I didn't. The hardest thing for me to get over was that my parents never talked about sex. If they said anything, it was negative. They never, ever said, "It's okay. It's good." Sex was always bad. For example, my mother gave me a menstruation kit and took the tampons out because "you don't wear tampons. You might lose your virginity that way." Knowing the background I come from and the way my parents always talked about sex being gross, I don't see how I am even seminormal.

In addition to the negative picture of sex painted in the home, Nancy had two early sexual encounters with adult males while she was a child. The first occurred, not with her father, but with a middle-aged farm hand who worked on her father's farm. The feelings and reaction she had to this encounter would be repeated the following year in similar experiences with her father.

N: I was about five years old, and I was petrified of this man anyway. He touched me sexually and told me that he would kill me if I ever told. Every time I would see him I would run the other way. The first time it happened, I was in the barn. The second time I was in a field. My dad was irrigating, and we were running under the water. I happened to come out at the end of the row, and this man was the only one there. It happened again. I was petrified to tell anyone, especially my family. . . .

With my dad, it happened in my parents' bed. They used to have all of us come spend the night in the bed between them. I think now that they had us sleep with them in order to avoid having sexual activity. My parents always invited each of us, not just me. . . . I remember when I was old enough to begin to understand what my father was doing, I hated it. My dad would ask me to spend the night with them. I started saying "No." My mother would come and ask me "Why don't you want to spend the night with us?" I would just tell her something like, "I just don't want to sleep with anyone. I want to stretch out in bed by myself." At that point, the molestation never happened again. My father never said another word. . . .

I am pretty sure that my mother never knew what happened between my father and I because he would plan it so we would be to bed before my mother. She was not in the bed with us at the time my dad would touch me.

In thinking about each of the children being invited to sleep in the parents' bed, Nancy wondered if perhaps her only sister was also approached by their father. Because neither of her parents knew about the farmhand, and her mother does not know about the father's molestation, Nancy thinks it is possible that the same thing happened to her sister.

N: I feel really bad that I never asked my sister if anything like that happened to her. You know, if he did anything to her, too. I really think she would tell me if he had, but then again, she may feel guilty if she thinks that he didn't do it with me, too. I have often wondered if I should even bring it up with her.

Nancy also felt the subject was taboo to discuss with her friends while she was growing up. Even now, she has told only five people of the experience with her father.

N: When I was in high school, I did have two good girlfriends. We were like the Three Stooges. I never even told them about my dad. I was afraid to tell them because I thought *I* had done something wrong— that maybe somehow it was all *my* fault. Also, I was afraid people would say, "How can you still call him a neat person?" or "How can you still care for him?" I didn't want people to think that.

Although they have not discussed it in the intervening twenty-one years, the fondling still affects the relationship between Nancy and her father.

N: I can't remember the last time my father and I kissed. I don't like for him to hug me. I have never felt comfortable around him. I am uncomfortable when I come into the same room with him and it is just the two of us.

I: Is part of the uncomfortable feeling not knowing how or what he thinks about what happened between you?

N: Yes, wondering that and why he did what he did and why he never hugged me right when I was a little kid. He'll bring up things I can't even remember doing and tell me how proud he is of me. I have actually said to him, "Why didn't you say this when I was a kid?" I needed to hear it from him. I needed it from both of my parents.

I: Have you ever had a desire to talk to your father about what happened?

N: Yes, but it is fear that keeps me from doing that—fear of wondering how I would treat him afterwards. Part of it is fear of hurting my mom. It would absolutely tear her apart if she found out. She would probably have a nervous breakdown. I guess maybe I knew that at the time. Maybe that is part of the reason why I never told anyone, or maybe it is all of the reason. I never told my mom, she couldn't deal with it.

Sexuality plays a large role in her thoughts now. Part of it is curiosity, and part of it is trying to make some sense of her experiences.

N: I have sat down and wondered what it would be like to go to bed with a woman. I don't think I could ever do it; I have never tried it, but I don't think it is as cut and dried as everyone thinks. Some of my best friends at work are "gay." My father would think I had lost my mind if he knew I had gay friends. He would probably say, "I always thought you were a weird cookie in our family, and now I know." Even though I have proven myself competent professionally and academically, I still think the only way I can be in control of what is happening is sexually. If I know a man is attracted to me sexually, then I can say, "No." When that happens and they come on, I know I have the little bastard right where I want him. I never felt that way with my husband, and that was weird for me. But, he has never pushed sex.

Questions about her sexuality and what is "normal" and what is not normal played a major role in Nancy's decision to have children. She had established herself well enough in her career so it was possible for her to take some time to have a baby and then be able to resume the career she enjoys. She thoroughly enjoys her nine-month-old daughter, but there were, and still remain, some doubt.

N: I did have this fear that if I did have a weird sense about sex, I didn't want to pass that on to my children. I am still . . . there are still times when . . . if Dick [her husband] were to approach me sexually, I would say "No." Like I don't want him coming on like it's a demand or he is in control. . . .

I particularly did not want to have a daughter. I still have fears. I still don't know if I will handle her right. I don't want anything like the fondling to happen to her. But, if it ever does, I want her to feel it is okay to talk to me about it. There's a fine line between being an "open" mother and being too much of a best friend. It's going to be hard for me to remember where that line is. But, right now, I wouldn't give anything in the world for having a girl. I am so excited when I see her and Dick together. I think what a neat relationship they have and are going to have in the future. I wish that I had had that with my father. They are going to be so close!

Nancy's Dating Relationships

Although Nancy dated occasionally throughout high school, it was not until she went away to college that her social life really developed. She was popular and dated frequently. She had girlfriends, but most of these relationships were with the girls in her sorority. It was during this time that she had her first sexual experience as an adult.

N: I dated a guy I really cared about all through college. We grew up together. I was almost nineteen, and one night I looked at him and said, "I'm tired of being a virgin." He said, "You are not going to use me. You don't just go to bed with me because you are tired of being a virgin." It ended up that he was the first guy I went to bed with. He's gay now. I didn't know anything about gays at the time. People would say stuff about him, but I just thought he respected me is why we didn't have sex earlier. He is still the greatest person there ever was. He is a terrific guy. I give him shit about being gay.

After this initial sexual relationship, Nancy became aware of not knowing how she felt sometimes or who she was. Her second serious relationship also occurred while she was in college.

N: I dated I don't know how many guys, but I always felt that I had to be in control of the sexual activity. I may have gone to bed with them, but I could cut them off the next day. I mean very easily, too! I kept so many feelings locked up because I did not know *how* to care, *how* to talk, *how* to feel. I didn't know what I was *supposed* to do. No one had ever said to me "Nancy, just however you feel—that's okay." . . .

I was always in control of the sexual activity. If I didn't want it, "Don't fuck with me, buddy." You know, sometimes that was the end of the relationship. I could let go—bam! . . .

I started dating a guy in college who was really good looking. As I look back, I think he must have been mentally disturbed. He was insanely jealous! He convinced me that I looked slutty because I was a Little Sister for one of the fraternities. I didn't really date any of them in the fraternity. All of my best friends have always been guys. Basically, I don't like women. Anyway, every time I would go to the frat house, everyone would hug my neck. It was really nothing. But, this guy went berserk and said I looked slutty for doing that. He had really convinced me that it probably was not the best thing to do. . . .

When it really hit me that the guy was nuts was when he tried to turn me against my parents. My parents had never said anything about anyone I had dated; they felt that it was my choice. But, one day, my mom came to me and said, "Nancy, Bernie is not the one for you because you can't be yourself with him. You don't cut up anymore. You have gotten withdrawn. You are just not the same person around him." I listened but I really didn't pay too much attention until Bernie tried to turn me against them. I don't know why he didn't like my parents or my whole family. I think he was just jealous. I finally got the message that he was the one who was nuts, not me. I broke it off.

Nancy's Marriage

After graduating from college, Nancy moved to Atlanta and began to work in a large advertising agency. It was here that she met her future husband.

> N: One day the receptionist at work told me, "Have I got the perfect guy for you." Now this lady was sitting there as sweet as she could be, but with a *huge* beehive hairdo. I was thinking to myself that I didn't think I would be attracted to a guy she would like. But, she kept telling me about him and saying that when he got back into town, we would meet, fall in love, and get married. I just thought this was one weird lady. But, about two weeks later, I was in the Xerox room working and this guy came walking in. I thought that he was cute, and then something inside of me said, "Nancy, meet your future husband." It was real clear to me. You know, you don't believe those things when you hear about them. But, it happened this was the same guy the receptionist had been talking about. Ten weeks later we were engaged. Eight months later we were married, and that was six years ago.

Meeting and marrying Dick was not a priority on Nancy's agenda at this time. She was excited about her career, living in Atlanta, and her future. She never thought she ever wanted to marry.

> N: When I met Dick, I was really heavy duty into my career. I never really thought I would marry at all. I didn't want to. When we talked about it, I told him right off the bat I didn't want to have kids. I was real bitter about the life my mother has led, even though I really blame her because she could have changed it. It was her choice. But, my mother is so meek and mild she needed my father's strength. He just treated her like another child. She was really his seventh child. My mother has never had a life of her own. I don't think to this very day that she knows who she is or what *she* wants out of life. I had this idea that once you married, you were chained and you would never grow.

Nancy says that there was something different in their relationship right from the start. It was almost eerie that Dick knew exactly how to approach her and had almost a sixth sense about not pushing her, especially in the sexual area.

N: We dated for about a month almost every night. We still had not made love. After about ten dates he told me, "Nancy, I would really love to make love with you, but only when you are ready." It was like someone had sat him down and said, "If you really want her to be attracted to you . . . this is what you need to do. . . . You need to handle her with care and don't push sex." We never talked about sex, and he never pushed it. He never even tried it. We could have sat and kissed for ten hours, and he would never have pushed for anything more. He has since said that that was just how he felt about me. He cared so much for me so early, he didn't want to do anything to lose me. Since he was twenty-eight and I was twenty-two, he didn't want to scare me off or have me think that he was too old for me. Another thing that really attracted me to him was that we were always doing fun things. He was really the first person in my life that I was not afraid to let go and care about. But I thought he was going to dump me, and I had always been the one to dump the guys. . . .

Also, Dick is so different from anyone I had ever known. He is probably one of the best human beings on the face of the earth. I really don't deserve the guy. I really don't understand how or why he is with me . . . because I am not the best person in the world. I haven't led a blemish-free life. But he is so good to me. I think my father is jealous of Dick. He really likes Dick, but he is jealous of our relationship. Dick is so caring, yet he is so strong. So willing to help me, but he doesn't try to control me. We have a very equal relationship.

After a courtship of two and a half months, Nancy invited Dick home with her for Thanksgiving dinner. Although she had some reservations about this invitation, she extended it, and Dick asked her what had taken her so long.

N: I guess in some ways I have always been a little embarrassed for friends to meet my family because I am so different from them. They are all real small-town folks. We live in a huge home on a lake and all this, but they are still basically "country." I didn't take most of the people home that I dated. . . .

We had a big, fancy Thanksgiving dinner, and then on the way back to Atlanta, Dick didn't say a word. I was thinking, "Oh shit. I knew it. I can't believe I did this. I really blew it!" I decided I would be the one who ended our relationship first—that I wouldn't give him the chance to hurt me. We stopped by his house on the way to my apartment, and he fixed us some drinks. He still hadn't said much, and I was very nervous. I was still thinking of a way to call off our relationship before he did. The next thing I knew, he asked me to marry him.

Although she felt some embarrassment about her family, they were the first ones Nancy called to announce her engagement. Her father was quick to voice reservations about the marriage, and the ongoing struggle between father and daughter continued.

N: My dad said, "Now, Nancy, you haven't really known this young man for very long." I wouldn't let him spoil it for me. I told him "I will have known him seven months when we marry. You only knew Mother for six weeks."

This lack of communication between Nancy and her parents continued until the wedding. Being from a small town and the daughter of one of the leading families, Nancy had a wedding that was considered a real "happening" in the small hometown. The night before the wedding her mother wanted to sit down and tell her the facts of life. Nancy told her to "forget it." But other areas were open to argument and a struggle for control.

N: My mom and I argued constantly about my wedding. I told her the girls in the wedding party would be wearing pink-gauze, street-length dresses that were off the shoulder. I told her that to go with their dresses, I wanted to wear an off-white gown. She was going to make my wedding gown, and she said, "I am not going to make it off-white. Do you know what you are telling the world if you don't wear white? You *will* wear white." I finally just said, "Forget it. It's your wedding anyway." . . .

Another thing we argued about was champagne. We had a knock-down fight about that. She said, "None of my friends will come if you have that." I said, "None of my friends will come if we don't!" So, we had champagne. And if the food was right here, the champagne was *way* over there. My mother doesn't have a mean bone in her body, but sometimes she walks around like an ostrich with her head in the sand.

Dick was and is the stabilizing force in Nancy's life. He is the middle of three children, having an older brother who is forty and a younger sister who is twenty-seven. He has very close ties to his family. He comes from a very traditional, tight-knit, middle-class family. His father graduated number one in his college class in electrical engineering at nineteen years old. His mother is, and always has been, a housewife, but with a mind of her own. Nancy has grown very close to Dick's family.

N: Dad is in sales. He has been very successful and probably could have been even more so, but he doesn't like anyone telling him what to do. He is also an alcoholic. Actually, our fathers are very much alike. A big difference is that Dick's father married a much stronger woman than my father. Mom is the neatest lady you will ever meet. She has spunk and wants to stay on top of things, but she still wants to be Mom. She's very good, but she doesn't take any shit. We are very close. The only thing that makes me angry about her is when she pretends that Dad doesn't have a drinking problem. He can be a real jerk when he is drunk.

In Dick's parents, Nancy has found strong role models. She loves them, but can stand back enough to be objective while evaluating their strengths and weaknesses. She finds her mother-in-law a friend and enjoys being the favorite daughter-in-law of both of them.

N: In Daddy's eyes, I can do no wrong. Part of the reason is that our dads are so much alike. I can say things to Dick's father that I wish I could say to mine. I can be very honest with him. Like sometimes, I just say, "Eat shit, Buddy." . . .

He's partial to me, and he is also partial to our daughter. Sometimes it really gets embarrassing because he has another granddaughter also. He says that Monica has a special smile just for him.

On the surface, Dick and Nancy came from two loving, long-term families of origin. To others they appeared to be the all-American families. Nancy realized earlier in life that her family was living a lie—that there is no such thing as a "perfect" family. For Dick, this realization came after they were married.

N: It took Dick several years to admit that his father was an alcoholic just like mine—that he didn't come from quite the perfect family he wishes for. His brother and father used to get into actual fistfights. His sister and father don't really get along. It's only been recently that Dick has been able to confront his dad about his drinking. It was a *big* thing in our marriage to get Dick to go to Al-Anon meetings with me.

For Nancy, the marriage was the beginning of a union in which she has grown in her understanding of love and acceptance of the idea that she is lovable. Moreover, it opened many new challenges for the girl from the small, southern town. A month before their marriage, Dick's position with the advertising firm was abolished when the account he was working on was moved to another agency. Losing his job proved to be a mixed blessing for the couple.

> N: I was dying to move to New York. That is like the Hollywood of advertising. I wanted to go so badly, but I don't think I would have ever moved there by myself. I told Dick after he lost his job, "Why don't we move up there . . . we have no ties, nothing stopping us." So, we rented our house to another couple and moved in an apartment in New York City.

The move opened many new experiences for Nancy. She and Dick made new friends. Both got positions with advertising agencies and soon adapted to a completely new lifestyle.

> N: One thing that I loved about New York was you could do whatever you wanted, and no one thought you were goofy because everyone was doing their own thing. I have never known such freedom.

Nancy also felt that she had finally hit her stride professionally. She was employed by the second largest advertising firm in the world and felt she was sinking her teeth into what she really wanted to do with her life. She said the freedom to just "be herself" was a new feeling. It made the idea of returning to the South and her old way of life very undesirable.

However, Dick was not as satisfied in New York as he had expected to be. He became anxious to return to Atlanta. A lucrative job offer for Dick soon loomed as a giant problem for the marriage.

> N: When Dick first told me of this new job offer, I told him my career did not warrant us staying in New York. He was making two and half times more than I was, and his career was ten years further down the road than mine. I really struggled with the move. We came to Georgia for Christmas that year, and on the way back to New York, I told him it was okay with me for him to accept the new job. . . .
>
> When he came home one night and told me that he had accepted the job in Atlanta, I felt like my stomach had fallen out. As it got closer and closer to the time for me to leave, I knew I couldn't do it because it would be going completely against my belief to go back. I told Dick I realized that I would be moving because I was "Mrs. Nancy Jones," not because I was just "Nancy." I also told him that I knew I would be *real* unhappy moving back and that I would make him

unhappy, too. So, he moved in January, and I stayed in our apartment and kept my job.

Nancy has described Dick as being almost perfect. She says he is the "most loving, most sensitive, caring person" in the world. She began to feel that she was not perfect, and therefore she did not deserve this wonderful marriage. Her career became a focal point of their arguments.

> N: Dick was in love with me. I think he thought when we married that all of my career plans would just fly out of the window, and we would have our own Ozzie and Harriet relationship. I told him I knew he was trying hard to be supportive of my career, but in essence he really wasn't behind me. I felt I was always pushing him. He never pushed me. I felt like I had to keep fighting to get what I wanted, and I knew I couldn't continue to live that way.

For two months Dick and Nancy lived with the long-distance marriage, with him in Atlanta and her in New York. She said she even found herself trying to discourage him. At night when the telephone rang and she knew it was him calling, she intentionally would not answer the phone so he would think she was out.

A close relationship developed between Nancy and her mentor. After two months, Nancy knew it was time to reevaluate her position on marriage.

> N: That March, I guess I began to understand "love." I mean, I said I loved Dick, and I thought I did. He was basically a guy I could be with and say and do whatever I wanted to do. I could be in control, but not too much in control. My boss took me to dinner one night and told me I was a "basket case." He wanted to know when I was going to hand in my resignation and move to Atlanta. I told him I wasn't. . . .
>
> The previous summer, Dick and I had flown to Atlanta and bought a motorcycle, which we rode back up to New York. I had pictures of that trip on my desk at the office. My boss said he thought it was neat that two people really alike had found each other and could have their own careers and yet help one another also. I told him that was the problem. We couldn't really be together, in our own careers, and then be interested in each other's career, too. . . .
>
> My boss and I started having dinners together. I almost fell in love with him. He did fall in love with me, even though it started out with him trying to help me get myself together. The day I was leaving New York, he called and asked me to stay. He said if money was the

problem, I could have whatever I wanted. I said that wasn't it. I had to come to Atlanta to try and work things out with Dick. It was probably the hardest thing I ever did. . . .

I realized that I must really care for Dick. With my boss, I kept hearing my father in the background saying, "na na na . . . you are just like all other women. A typical woman." But I hated myself for coming back down here. Part of me was glad to be back with Dick, but part of me resented leaving New York. We were real miserable the first year I was back.

There were many ups and downs that first year, including Nancy's decision to move out, separate, and get an apartment on her own. Although Dick did not understand why Nancy was so unhappy, he was nonetheless willing to give her whatever space she felt she needed to work things out. She was worried that if she moved out, people would think she was crazy because she actually could give no reason, just a general sense of unhappiness.

N: It was the same uncomfortable feeling that I get when I go back to my hometown. I get real depressed, even today. I hate the place! When I went to college, I was doing all the "right" things and being very much the "southern belle." When we moved to New York, all of my liberal side came out and I loved it! The things we would sit around and talk about, or the things I would do, or the feelings I had . . . I just loved them all. I was *very* happy there. When we moved back to Atlanta, I thought we were regressing. I hated it. Once we decided to move back, I made up my mind I would not call or see or have anything to do with our old friends. If we were going to be back in Atlanta, I was going to treat it as a whole different, new town. I really felt bad because Dick was so excited. We have a lot of mutual friends, and so they all knew through him when I was back. When we socialized, I would just sit there because I had grown out of this silly stage I think some of them still live in. What's really bad is that when I am with them, I just go along with them. I can walk into a room and be just as silly. I think that is one problem I have always had in having girlfriends. I am not silly. I can be silly sometimes and cut up and joke, but I have always found it hard to play the silly little girl role. That was one of the main reasons I didn't want to come back, because I thought I would have to be a certain way.

Nancy never did move out permanently, and she and Dick had been married for six years at the time of the interview. Their nine-month-old daughter has added a new dimension to their lives. Dick is still very willing to give Nancy her "space."

N: Sometimes I feel guilty. I feel bad, I feel sad. I really pray that my mother could have just a little bit of happiness. When I see the relationship that I have with my husband and the relationship he has with Monica, and the relationship the three of us will have as she grows up . . . that's really all my mother ever asked for. That's not a whole lot to ask for in this life. Sometimes it just doesn't seem fair. I hit the gold mine. It seems that things have always just come very easy for me, and I don't understand why. Even when I was pregnant, I never had morning sickness. I was really never sick one day. I jogged daily until I was six months along. I walked three miles the morning she was born. I had total natural childbirth. Afterwards I thought I just must have had a very easy time because I didn't think it was as bad as everyone had always said it would be. The pain was awful, don't get me wrong. I threw up about fifty times. What I found out later was that I had had a very difficult time, but it wasn't to me what it was to other people. I diminish my own accomplishments. I think maybe in my own way, maybe making myself grow up early and handle things that I did, I can deal with pain a lot more easily than other people.

Nancy's life may seem complete—an adoring husband, a beautiful daughter, and a lovely home, plus the freedom to do whatever she wants. Yet, Nancy is still haunted with questions about where her life is going.

N: I worry that something is going to happen to me. I guess I just feel unworthy to have all this. Sometimes I have wondered if part of me would not love a catastrophe so that I could just release all of the feelings I have always kept inside.

I: Do you feel you need a catastrophe to be justified in releasing or showing your emotions?

N: Yeah, I guess so. There are times when Monica is asleep, and I decide she is dead. I go back into her room and just stare at her, or I pop her on the butt to see her wiggle. Just to see if she is alive. Or sometimes if I go out for a drink with a friend and I get a call from Dick's office, I just know he has been in an accident. That he is dead. Then I wonder, unconsciously, do I really want something like that to happen? Am I wishing for something like that so I can be released from the part of this life that I don't like? It's weird because I don't honestly know if I am really happy, or just won't let myself be happy, or if I am not happy and I won't go after what's missing. One of the things I thought about when I was thinking about leaving Dick and moving into an apartment was, "Well, I will be in a mess a year from now if I realize I was happy and he's gone."

Nancy's Future

Being at home as a full-time mother and homemaker is something Nancy never thought she would do, much less enjoy. It took her more than a year to get pregnant once she decided to have a child. Then, in her own words, it became a goal to get pregnant because she became very angry that it had taken so long to conceive. Although she took only six weeks' leave from her career, it has stretched into more than nine months as she realized that she is not really a "Kinder Care mom." The Christmas season brought many opportunities for her to display her skills around her home.

> N: All Christmas, all I did was sit and cross-stitch. For gifts I gave all of my nieces and nephews personalized Christmas ornaments. I made all of the decorations around the house. There was not a room in this house that wasn't decorated. It looked like something out of *Southern Living*. When I look around, I realize that there are not many people who can do the things I do. And I can't imagine not having this wonderful daughter who is half me and half Dick.

However, Nancy admits that she is getting an "itch" to go back to her career. Although no plans are final, she is beginning to think about her return. She feels a big part of her is missing by not balancing motherhood with her career. She does admit that she may like telling people she works in advertising more than she likes the actual day-to-day work.

> N: Basically I am a peon in the company. I am in the marketing end of the advertising business. I deal directly with the clients. Sometimes I get caught in the middle. The client bitches about the product, and then the agent bitches at me because we have a shithead client who can't see the value of the product. But, I love it! I am always balancing . . . which goes back to my taking care of everyone. Even though I am a peon, I have a great insight into people, why they act as they do, what their motives are. I am really surprising at reading people. Sometimes I can almost tell what they are thinking. I can sit there and work with a person for a week and *know* I have to be a certain way to sell that person. It really pays off when you are presenting copy. I can present it in ten different ways in order to get ten different points across. Whatever vibes I am getting from the person is what I present.

Her husband has left the decision of whether to resume her career or not up to her. Although he is inclined to prefer her to stay home and be a full-time mother, he has told her that it is her decision. Although Nancy knows she has great freedom in her marriage, there are still many questions that remain unanswered.

N: It is very hard for me to show my emotions to anybody. To really care. Sometimes, even now, I don't think I love like I should. I don't know if I even truly *know* the meaning of love. I care about Dick, I really do. I love him. But sometimes these thoughts go through my mind, like, "I don't really want this life. Why am I pretending to live this life?" Part of me at times wants to be a beatnik and just go and do and say "Screw the world! I don't really care." But, I have *always* done the *right* thing. What I need is my ass kicked. I work hard for things, but then when I get them, I don't appreciate them like I should. I tell myself that 99.9 percent of the women in the world would love to have what I have. If someone sat down and wrote out what they were looking for in a mate, you couldn't ask for a better person than my husband. . . .

Dick would never hurt me, and that is what bothers me. I am not 100 percent sure that I won't end up hurting him. I would never do it on purpose. One reason I never moved out when we talked about separating is that I didn't want to hurt him. I will let myself suffer to keep everyone else happy.

Again, Nancy sees herself in a state of flux.

N: Part of me is still unhappy. I don't know why. What am I supposed to do? Sometimes I think maybe I would enjoy going back to work in advertising, and other times I think I would enjoy going back to school so I could eventually work with abused children. I have thought about doing some volunteer work with abused children to see if I would really like it or not.

Also, there are some regrets that mayby she did not break out of the mold of always "doing the right thing" and just go in whatever direction her life might take.

N: I guess if I could change anything, I wish I had done some of the things I thought were crazy and then just lived through the consequences. When I was in high school, all I wanted to do was graduate and be a missionary. I wanted to go overseas and help the poor. My father thought . . . well, there was never any discussion. Part of me wanted to do it, but something in me wouldn't let me. And things like when I got out of college I *had* to have a job with such and such an advertising agency. Nothing else would do. What I *really wanted* to do was to take a job as a flight attendant for a while. I had the option to do that, but I said no . . . I was a marketing major, and I wouldn't let myself get into anything else. I was very goal-oriented. Everything has always had to be what other people thought was right.

Finally, when asked what advice she might give to a younger girl who is currently experiencing or has previously experienced a sexual relationship with her own father, Nancy says:

N: My advice is to be your own self. Let your feelings come through. For a while I was afraid of giving my opinions, afraid that certain things I was thinking would be considered weird, that I would be out of the norm. My father used to always instill in me, "Be your own self," and "Stand on your own two feet." Yet, when I tried to do that, he would beat me down because he wanted to carry me around in his hip pocket. I feel I have always had to fight for things, and I don't know where I got the strength to fight my father, but I did. . . .

I have found out that there are a lot of weird people out there who are considered "normal." People pass things off as their idiosyncrasy. If you really got into their backgrounds, you would probably find that some of them who appear normal, although they did not go through a childhood sexual molestation, may have been exposed to other, more damaging things. But you don't do studies on those things.

Two years after the interviews were completed, Nancy read the final version of the chapter on her life. Many changes had taken place in her life during that time.

A great source of joy for her has been the birth of a second daughter, Margaret, who was five months old at the completion of the project.

Nancy has had the opportunity to talk with her only sister about the sexual contact between herself and their father. Her sister revealed that the father had also sexually approached her. She, too, was able to tell him "no" and stop the abuse. However, the sister also revealed that when she was a teen-ager, she had walked in on her father kissing one of her girlfriends.

Nancy's twenty-four-year-old brother, Bob, spent time with her and her family while he was going through a divorce after a six-year marriage to his high-school sweetheart. In their conversations about the marriage, Bob revealed to Nancy that one of the major problems had been his wife's sexual dysfunction as a result of being molested as a child by her father. Nancy decided that this was the opening she needed to reveal to her brother the sexual contact she had had with their father. She says that Bob was extremely understanding and supportive of her. He could immediately identify with the sexual problems that she and Dick have had to work out in their marriage. Nancy feels that by revealing her secret to her brother, they have only grown closer.

Nancy has also told an older brother about the molestation by the farm hand. Since he and their father are very close, she stopped short of telling him about the molestation by the father.

In summary, Nancy had this to say:

N: I realize how much better I understand my feelings than I did even two years ago. I am a much happier person now. I also understand my parents more. They were not the perfect parents I had created in my mind that they should have been. But I love them both very deeply. I always have. I just have to accept them the way they are. In their own right, they were great parents. They taught six children how to be good human beings. How to respect others. . . .

One day I will have to confront my father about the molestation. I want my two daughters to be able to visit without me worrying if something will happen to them. He and Monica are already real close. I do not want to destroy that relationship or prevent him from having one with Margaret. But, I will not let the same thing happen to them. I love my father and up until recently I was ashamed to say it. I thought "How could I love a father who molested his own daughter?" I don't understand it completely, but I truly believe that he never really meant to hurt me.

7
Results

This book marks the first major attempt to investigate through qualitative research the long-term consequences of a childhood sexual experience with one's father. Speculative articles have described many deleterious effects of such an experience. These hypothesized effects of a childhood sexual experience with the father and the child's later development might be best understood in the framework of Erikson's theory of psychosocial development (Erikson, 1950).

This chapter will present a brief overview of Erikson's stages of development. The demographic descriptors of each participant at the time of the interviews will be examined for similarities and differences. In reviewing the data, four primary relationships in each participant's life became significant in their completion of Erikson's psychosocial stages. These relationships were with: (1) their mothers, (2) their fathers, (3) their peers, and (4) their husband(s) or male companions. How these relationships contributed to the participants' completing or failing to complete Erikson's stages will be examined. The ages (26 to 28 years old) of the participants in this study eliminates comparison with Erikson's last two stages.

Erikson's Theory of Psychosocial Development

Erikson viewed development as a continuous process extending from birth through adulthood to old age. He describes human development in a series of eight stages. He calls them psychosocial stages because he believes that the psychological development of individuals depends on the social relations established at various points in life.

Erikson theorizes that there are special problems or conflicts that must be met at each stage. These conflicts must be resolved, at least to some extent, before the individual can go on to the next stage. Each stage is not passed through and left behind. Rather, each stage contributes to the formation of the total personality. While these stages are chronological, they are not laid out according to a strict timetable. And, although the stages are not based on scientific evidence, they do call attention to the kinds of problems people encounter during their lives.

Psychosocial Stages

According to Erikson's theory, the first conflict to be resolved in the healthy personality is *basic trust versus basic mistrust.* Feelings of trust in other people depend to a large extent on the way early needs were handled by the primary caregivers. Insensitive parenting or repeated separations may undermine a child's trust. Basic trust in self and others is necessary for human development. Inability to form an attachment to one or a few primary persons in the early years has been related to an inability to develop close interpersonal relationships in adulthood.

Erikson's second stage is *autonomy versus shame and doubt.* The task at this stage is to establish a will of one's own. The child learns from the self and from others what is expected and what is not expected. To the extent that parents encourage a child's sense of exploration and ability to do things independently, the child begins to develop a sense of independence and autonomy. The child begins to experience an autonomous will, asserting the self within the family. For a child to work through this stage successfully, the child must be treated with dignity and respect. The lack of developed autonomy can lead to feelings of shame, doubt, and unworthiness.

The third stage is *initiative versus guilt.* During this stage a child separates from the family of origin and widens his or her social world independently. While a close relationship with a warm and responsive adult is essential for a child's development, interaction with other children plays an important role, too. Without the opportunity to play with other children, the individual does not develop normal patterns of behavior. Parental attitudes—encouraging or discouraging—can make a child feel inadequate or guilty.

Erikson's stage of *industry versus inferiority* reflects a child's psychosocial dilemma of mastering tasks that are essential to functioning in society. Mastering experience forms the basis for a sense of competence. Without this sense, a child feels inferior. Children measure themselves against the standards of their peers.

The fifth stage is *identity versus identity confusion.* A major task confronting the adolescent is to develop a sense of identity—to find answers to the questions, "Who am I?" and "Where am I going?" The search for personal identity involves feelings about one's own worth and competence. Role confusion is the product of the adolescent's inability to identify adequately with others.

The final stage to be examined in this study is *intimacy versus isolation.*

During the adult years, people generally commit themselves to an occupation and marriage or form other types of intimate relationships. Intimacy here means an ability to care about others and to share experiences with them. People who cannot commit themselves to a loving relationship risk being isolated.

Demographic Descriptors

A comparison of selected demographic descriptors of the three participants at the time of the interviews is included in table 7–1. The three women are Caucasian and are between the ages of twenty-six and twenty-eight years. All other variables are different.

Susan appears to be the most different. One might hypothesize that the dissimilarities in education, religious faith, and outside support systems may contribute to differences in later life adjustment.

Table 7–1
Demographic Descriptors

Descriptor	Susan	Judy	Nancy
Age	28 years old	26 years old	28 years old
Race	Caucasian	Caucasian	Caucasian
Educational background	Completed 8th grade	B.S. college	B.S. business
Occupation	Unskilled, hourly wage (usually waitress)	Teacher	Advertising
Current marital status of parents	Divorced	Divorced	Divorced, remarried to each other
Number of siblings	Fourteen	Three	Five
Number of marriages	Three plus common-law relationships	Two	One
Number of children	Four	None	One daughter
Previous therapy experiences	None	Individual, marital, and group therapy	None
Role of religion in her life	Vague, sporadic	Active in church	Important, but not involved in organized church
Sexually abusive experiences other than with father	Maternal grandfather, raped by six black men, raped by friend's brother	None	Father's farm hand

Descriptors of Mothers

Similarities and Differences

An examination of table 7–2 suggests that the major differences in the subjects' relationships with their mothers were: the role religion played in the mothers' lives, their absences from the home, the amount of physical abuse they administered to their children, their extramarital relationships, their knowledge of the sexual contact between their husbands and daughters, and the current relationship between the mother and daughter.

Religion played no role in Susan's childhood, whereas Judy and Nancy came from families where religion was a focal point. Both Judy's mother and Nancy's mother frequently sought their own refuge in prayer. They insisted that their families attend Sunday services as well as be involved in other church-related activities.

Susan's mother was frequently absent from the home. These absences usually involved her current boyfriend. Judy's mother was also frequently absent because of hospitalizations resulting from her schizophrenia. Nancy's mother was never absent from the home for long periods of time.

Susan's mother was both physically and verbally abusive to her children. Judy and Nancy were never physically or verbally abused by their mothers.

Susan's mother was involved in many extramarital relationships. These affairs took place in the home and frequently with the children's knowledge. Men were often moved into the house while the father was stationed over-

Table 7–2
Descriptors of Mothers

Descriptor	Susan	Judy	Nancy
Occupation	Housewife	Housewife	Housewife
Educational background	Unknown	High school	High school
Extramarital relationships	Many	None	None
Absences from the home	Frequent with men	Frequent hospitalizations	None
Physical abuse of children	Beatings with belts and broom handles	None	None
Role of religion in her life	None	Important	Important
Knowledge of sexual contact between husband and daughter	Yes	Yes	No
Relationship with daughter today	None, does not know where she is	Continued role reversal. Mother generally initiates	Continued role reversal. Daughter initiates frequent contact

seas. As far as Judy and Nancy know, their mothers have never had extramarital relationships.

Both Susan's mother and Judy's mother knew of the sexual relationship between their husband and daughter and did nothing to stop it, or to try to intervene and protect their daughters. Nancy is sure that her mother never knew of the sexual contact between herself and her father.

Today the relationships between the mothers and daughters differ greatly. Susan has no contact with her mother. She is not sure whether her mother is alive or dead and expresses no interest either way. She openly expresses anger and hatred toward her mother and feels that her mother is equally responsible, with her father, for the cycle of failure she has experienced in her life.

Judy reports feeling more at peace with her mother now that she is an adult. She reports that she has gained a better understanding of schizophrenia and thinks of her mother as being sick. This has allowed Judy not to hold her mother responsible for what happened and for her mother's inability or unwillingness to protect her. She has been able to accept her mother's limitations as a mother. She expresses no anger or hatred toward her mother. Judy's mother usually initiates any contact between them. Typically the role reversal continues, with the mother calling to seek advice.

Nancy reports the best relationship with her mother of the three. While she expresses anger toward her mother for her helplessness in relation to the father, she still describes her as a "neat" lady. She frequently initiates contact with her mother and often visits her.

Relationship to Erikson's Stages

The women's relationships with their mothers (table 7–2) help elucidate the degree of completion they experienced in relation to Erikson's first two stages of development. The differences that emerge from the data help to account for the varying degrees of trust that were breached, as well as the degree of autonomy that was developed.

In relation to the first stage, *trust versus mistrust,* all three women felt betrayed by their mothers on some level. Perhaps most important, both Judy's and Susan's mothers knew of the sexual relationship between their husbands and daughters and did nothing to intervene. Therefore, not only did the daughters feel they had no control over the sexual contact, but they also experienced that they could not trust their mothers to control it, either.

The frequent absences of Judy's and Susan's mothers from the home also undermined the level of trust established. Susan's mother continued this undermining of trust by lying to her children and to her husband about her sexual relationships outside the marriage. While Nancy's mother may have lacked parenting skills, she was in the home and available to her children.

Susan's level of trust was handicapped further by her mother's verbal and physical abuse. This abuse, administered in a seemingly random fashion, helped contribute to a sense of helplessness and confusion.

Nancy most successfully completed Erikson's second stage, *autonomy versus shame and doubt*. She was able to stop the sexual contact with her father herself. This appears to have given her a sense of control in her life as well as the ability to assert herself. She was also allowed more freedom to become involved with people and activities outside the home.

In all three cases there was a complete role reversal between the mothers and daughters. For various reasons the mothers became dependent on the daughters. The daughters assumed many of the household duties as well as the care and supervision of younger siblings. This transfer of household responsibilities for Susan and Judy eventually included the sexual role. Nancy again was more assertive and rebellious in assuming these duties.

The role reversal between mother and daughter forced the daughter to fulfill obligations that were inappropriate for her age and, more importantly, that interfered with her normal maturation.

Descriptors of Fathers

Similarities and Differences

Table 7–3 indicates the differences in the participants' reports of their relationships with their fathers. The major differences among the fathers are: the educational level, the type of employment, their extramarital relationships, their physical abuse of their children, the length of sexual contact with their daughter, the type of sexual contact, how the relationship terminated, and the relationship between father and daughter today.

Susan's father completed high school and made a career as an enlisted man in the army. Both Judy's and Nancy's fathers graduated from college. Judy's father also graduated from law school, practiced law successfully, and owned his own firm. Nancy's father is a few hours short of completing a doctoral degree. He has been a successful large-scale farmer. He has also been elected county school superintendent for three terms.

Susan's and Judy's fathers had extramarital relationships that were known to the families. Nancy does not think her father ever had an extramarital affair.

There are important differences in the sexual relationships each woman had with her father. Susan actually experienced two periods of sexual contact with her father. The first period began when she was eight years old. This relationship continued for several years until she was taken out of the home and placed in a foster home. At eight, she felt helpless to stop her father's

Table 7–3
Descriptors of Fathers

Descriptor	Susan	Judy	Nancy
Educational background	High school	College and law school	College and graduate work
Occupation	Enlisted man, army	Attorney	Large-scale farmer, county school superintendent
Physical abuse of children	Beatings with fists	None	None
Extramarital relationships	Many	Many	None
Age of daughter when sexual contact began	8 years old	5 years old	6 years old
Length of relationship with daughter	Several years beginning at age 8; Several months at age 14 until she got pregnant	12 years	Episodic for one-and-a-half years
Type of sexual contact	Mutual masturbation, oral sex, intercourse	Mutual masturbation, oral sex, intercourse	Fondling, inappropriate kissing
How relationship ended	Pregnancy and marriage to another man	High school boyfriend installed lock on her bedroom door	She stopped it
Relationship between father and daughter	No contact, does not know where he is	Sporadic, he initiates	Frequent, she initiates
Sexual contact with other children in family	Attempts with older daughter	No other daughters	Younger sister

advances. She repeatedly told teachers, social workers, and a judge what was happening in the home. No one believed her or acted on this information. After being released from a reform school when she was thirteen, she sought her father out, as she had no place else to live. The sexual contact resumed progressing from masturbation and oral sex to intercourse. She became pregnant with her father's child when she was fourteen years old. The relationship between father and daughter was terminated when she moved out of the father's apartment.

Judy's relationship with her father lasted continuously for twelve years and began when she was five years old. Although it started with inappropriate kissing and fondling, it progressed to mutual masturbation, oral sex, and eventually to intercourse. While her father was not otherwise violent with her, he did threaten that if her mother learned of the relationship, she would have another nervous breakdown and have to be hospitalized again. So, although Judy felt helpless in relation to her father, she felt responsible for her mother. While she tried to stop her father's advances and sexual behavior throughout the twelve years, she internalized at an early age that she was powerless to do so. The relationship ended when she confided in a high-school boyfriend, who immediately installed a dead-bolt lock on her bedroom door. The boyfriend's actions were important for two reasons. First, it effectively put an end to the incest. Second, Judy was able to reveal the incest "secret" for the first time and not be rejected.

Nancy's relationship with her father was far less extensive. It lasted for a year and a half and consisted of inappropriate kissing and fondling. Possibly of major significance is the fact that Nancy herself was able to put a stop to the sexual contact. This appears to have given her a sense of confidence and a belief at an early age that she had control over what happened to her.

The relationships that exist between the fathers and daughters today are significant. Susan does not know where her father is. She expresses no interest in whether he is alive or dead. She openly expresses anger toward her father, but not hatred as with her mother. Judy's contact with her father is sporadic at best. He generally initiates it, often when he is drinking. She visits him approximately twice a year when she returns to her mother's home for the holidays. Since she considers her father sick, she has been able to forgive him to some degree. Nancy has the most frequent contact with her father. She often initiates this contact and visits him.

Relationship to Erikson's Stages

After reviewing the data, it is my opinion that the major psychological difficulty encountered by these three women can be traced to the father's violation of the child's trust. This failure to resolve Erikson's first psychosocial stage successfully has had negative consequences for their later development.

Susan's experience with this stage is the least complete. Her father's frequent absences from the home and his seemingly random physical abuse undermined the development of trust.

The chronic marital discord greatly colored each daughter's view of heterosexual interaction. The extramarital affairs of Judy's and Susan's fathers contributed not only to their inability to trust their fathers, but also to the growing sense of shame and guilt they felt resulting from their sexual contact with their fathers.

Nancy appears to have completed stage two, *autonomy versus shame and doubt,* more successfully than the other two women. Not only was the sexual contact with her father less extensive, but also she was able to stop the sexual contact herself. This appears to have strengthened her sense of autonomy. Also, since the sexual contact did not progress past inappropriate kissing and fondling, she does not appear to have developed the same degree of shame and doubt.

Susan (at eight years old) and Judy felt helpless to stop the sexual contact. They both internalized at an early age that their fathers' behavior was somehow their fault. The length of the sexual contact, the sexual behaviors involved, and—in Susan's case—the pregnancy, contributed to the degree of shame, doubt, and guilt that Judy and Susan felt.

Judy's revealing of the incest secret to her boyfriend and his continued love and support may have been the basis for her eventually learning to trust others. She still internalized shame and doubts about the sexual relationship and her inability to assert herself in stopping it.

Descriptors of Peer Relationships

Similarities and Differences

The relationships with peers illustrate the degree of success each woman experienced in completing Erikson's next three stages: *initiative versus guilt, industry versus inferiority,* and *identity versus identity confusion.*

Table 7–4 reflects the major differences these women reported with peer relationships including: the amount of involvement in school and church activities, periods of promiscuity, drug and alcohol abuse, lesbian relationships, the sex of the majority of their friends, and the relationships they have with their siblings.

Susan's frequent moves to foster homes and reform schools combined with the lack of discipline in her family of origin contributed to her sporadic school attendance. Becoming pregnant and dropping out of school in the ninth grade prevented her from participating in high-school peer activities.

Both Judy and Nancy report high degrees of involvement in extracurricular activities throughout their school years. These activities were often seen by them as a way to stay out of their homes. Activities with church groups were also seen as an escape for Nancy and Judy, but not for Susan.

Unlike the other two women, Nancy does not report having a promiscuous period in her life. Judy reports that she went through such a period after her divorce. Susan has repeatedly been involved in such relationships, often as a paid prostitute.

While Nancy reports never abusing drugs or alcohol, Susan and Judy have abused them both. Judy used neither drugs nor alcohol at the time of the interviews, but did experiment with them during her first marriage and for a period after her divorce. Susan considers herself an alcoholic and has also experimented with drugs extensively. Most of the people she has been involved with have also abused drugs and alcohol.

Table 7–4
Descriptors of Peer Relationships

Descriptor	Susan	Judy	Nancy
Reported self-concept while growing up	Feeling "weird," "different," "not normal"	Same	Same
Involvement in school activities	Almost none	Extensive	Extensive
Involvement in church activities	None	Extensive	Extensive
Periods of promiscuity	Yes	Yes, after divorce	No
Drug experimentation	Extensive	During first marriage and after divorce	No
Alcohol abuse	Yes, continues today	During first marriage and after divorce	No
Lesbian relationships	Yes	No	No
Sex of majority of friends	Male	Male or female	Male
Relationship with siblings	None	Infrequent contact	Close relationships

Susan is the only one who reports being involved in a lesbian relationship. She has been involved off and on for several years with the same woman.

All three of the participants report having more male friends than female friends. Susan and Nancy report that they like males better than females. All of the women say that they felt much older than their female peers while growing up as a result of the sexual contact with their fathers. They did not want to play "little girl games." Through her involvement in an all-female therapy group for adults who were childhood victims of incest and through church activities, Judy is beginning to appreciate the value of having both male and female friends.

Adding to her isolation from peers, Susan has no contact with any of her fourteen siblings. She does not know where any of them are. Judy has limited contact with her brothers on her visits to her mother about twice a year. She reports that these relationships are superficial. Nancy enjoys a close relationship with each of her siblings and has frequent contact with them. She still finds herself advising them or taking care of them.

Relationship to Erikson's Stages

The failure to complete Erikson's next three stages—*initiative versus guilt, industry versus inferiority,* and *identity versus identity confusion*—is reflected in the relationships these women have experienced with their peers.

It is apparent that each of these women failed, in childhood, to develop a positive self-concept. They each describe growing up without a feeling of being "okay," but rather feeling from a very young age that they were "weird," "dirty," or "different" from others. They internalized a feeling that the sexual contact had somehow been their fault. This "secret" then became the core of their identity. The negative feelings of not being like other people interfered with their ability to get close to others. They developed guilt rather than initiative. For Judy and Susan, particularly, there were few interactions with other children. Therefore, they did not develop age-appropriate patterns of behavior.

Nancy and Judy were able to complete Erikson's stage of *industry versus inferiority* more completely than Susan. Since Susan dropped out of school in the ninth grade, she was unable to master many of the tasks essential to functioning in society. In addition to being able to measure themselves against the standards of their peers, both Nancy and Judy were able to receive positive reinforcement from teachers in high school. These positive appraisals helped increase positive feelings they had about themselves and their abilities.

During adolescence, a young person develops to sexual maturity, establishes an identity as an individual away from the family, and faces the task of deciding how to earn a living. Nancy and Judy were more successful in completing this stage than Susan.

Developing an identity is a continuous process. New responses are acquired as a function of both direct and indirect experiences with parents and other role models. Parents serve as a primary source of identification. Because of the sexual experiences with their fathers, each of these women has experienced sexual-identification confusion to some extent. In Susan's case, this was complicated further by her mother's sexual promiscuity. The lack of appropriate sex-role models for both males and females led to later confusion on the part of each of these women.

Susan has gone through a prolonged period of identity confusion. She has not experienced the successes in high school, college, and careers that the other two women have. She is the only one of the three who has not developed a sense of personal identity as an adult.

Descriptors of Husband(s) or Male Companions

Similarities and Differences

Table 7–5 suggests that the major differences in the husbands or male companions are: their level of education, their use of drugs and alcohol, their physical abuse of their wives, and the amount of emotional support they are able to offer the women.

Table 7–5
Descriptors of Husband(s) or Male Companions

Descriptor	Susan	Judy	Nancy
General age of males	Older	Older	Older
Educational background	High school or less	College	College
Occupation	Blue collar/ unskilled	Teacher	Advertising account executive
Their use of alcohol and/or drugs	Very abusive	First husband was abusive of both, second is not	Normal use of alcohol, no drugs
Physical abuse of spouses/mates	Frequent	First husband was abusive, second is not	None
Level of emotional support given to women	Low	High	High

Susan has been involved with many more men than either Judy or Nancy. Most of these men completed high school, but received no further education or vocational training. Therefore, they tend to be employed in blue-collar occupations. Judy and Nancy have dated and married men who completed college.

Susan and Judy, in her first marriage, have been involved with men who abused both drugs and alcohol. These men have also been physically and verbally abusive to them. Nancy has not had the same experiences with men.

The level of emotional support these men have been able to offer the women also varies greatly. Susan has typically felt little emotional support from the men in her life. However, she was able to share her past with her common-law husband and also with her current boyfriend. For the first time, she felt that she has been loved and accepted in spite of her past. The relationship with her current boyfriend affords her the support and stability she has not known in previous relationships.

Judy and Nancy are both married to men who know of their sexual contact with their fathers. While the husbands do not approve of the fathers' behavior, they have been able to be supportive of their wives. They have also been able to allow their wives to work out a relationship with her family of origin. Both of these men come from long-term, monogamous families of origin where traditional middle-class values are stressed.

Relationship to Erikson's Stages

The relationships with husband(s) or male companions illustrates the degree of completion these women have experienced in dealing with Erikson's stage of *intimacy versus isolation*. Their basic mistrust of men has made it very difficult for each of these women ever to become truly intimate with a male. Each at various times in her life has expressed little hope of attaining a rewarding relationship with a man, and yet each expresses a longing for the nurturance and care that such a relationship would provide.

It is my opinion that a crucial difference in the degree to which this stage has been completed is illustrated by the following fact: Nancy has not continued in abusive relationships with men, while Susan and Judy, until her second marriage, have. Susan and Judy both have had a tendency to choose men who are irresponsible, have poor impulse control, and have little respect for other people—much the same profile as their fathers. Many of their relationships have failed because they were based on their pathological parental role models. Having seen the mistreatment of their mothers, they have taken for granted that men will mistreat them also and that they will have no control in such relationships. Nancy seems to be the exception. She has been able to feel she has control in relationships with men.

Another major difference involves the attempts that Susan and Judy have made to recapture the nurturance and care they did not receive in childhood by participating in promiscuous sexual behaviors. One might see the promiscuity as a response to the guilt each brought from childhood. Each has tried to punish herself by having sex with a variety of men. The promiscuous behavior was a means of self-degradation, while at the same time a way to seek, through sex, the affection they were missing in their lives.

A possible crucial difference has been that Susan and Judy have been involved with men who abused both drugs and alcohol. Susan is the only one of the three women who is an alcoholic herself. However, many of the men in her life are also alcoholics. Neither Judy, Nancy, nor their husbands abuse drugs or alcohol.

Finally, and perhaps most importantly, Judy and Nancy are currently involved in strong, loving, mutually supportive marriages. It appears that they have both found mates who accept them as they are and with whom they do not have to pretend. Sharing the incest secret and being accepted has made the secret less dirty and less powerful in their lives. While Susan could benefit from such a relationship, she appears to lack the interpersonal skills necessary to form such a relationship.

While none of the women has completed the *intimacy versus isolation* stage, Nancy and Judy appear to be in better positions to do so than does Susan. Their husbands know of the incest and still have been able to be loving and supportive. The husbands have continued to encourage each of the women to grow and are accepting and supportive of their wives' efforts to find the answer to the question, "Who am I?" Both of the husbands have also been willing to allow their wives the freedom to continue to work out their relationships with their families of origin.

8
Conclusions and Recommendations

Two of the major purposes of this book were: (1) to identify specific adult consequences of a childhood sexual experience with one's father and, (2) to compare the adjustment and personality characteristics of three women who had such an experience.

Because of the design and nature of this study and the richness of the data it has generated, it is reasonable to assume that the findings can be generalized more readily than if a purely statistical approach had been used. With this advantage in mind, yet within the confines of this study, several conclusions can be drawn.

Conclusions

It would be an exaggeration to state that women who experience a childhood sexual relationship with their fathers inevitably sustain permanent damage. There is nonetheless considerable evidence to suggest that child victims are more vulnerable to a number of pathological developments in later life, and that a considerable number of these victims suffer lasting harm.

The findings of this study are consistent with prior research showing the relationship between a childhood sexual experience with one's father and later development. Such a relationship does appear to increase the risk that the child will experience a variety of difficulties in later life. However, many circumstances determine the course of a child's development, and the effects of a single trauma, such as incest, may be exacerbated or offset by other aspects of the child's environment.

The data in this study point to the violation of a child's trust by an adult(s) as the basis for the major psychological difficulty that develops in later life. The participants in this study never fully completed Erikson's first stage of basic trust versus basic mistrust. These women not only felt betrayed by their fathers, but came to feel betrayed by their mothers as well. They reacted by not being able to trust males or females.

A second conclusion resulting from this study is that incest occurs in families that reflect long-standing family disorganization. Specifically, there is a marked role reversal between the mother and daughter. This reversal places the daughter in the role of an adult without giving her the opportunity to master normal developmental tasks.

Data from this study indicate that children who experience an incestuous relationship grow up devaluing themselves. The women in this study failed in childhood to develop a positive self-concept, which forms the basis upon which other positive learning experiences can be built. They reported feeling different and isolated from their peers from an early age. They had feelings of being "dirty," "evil," or "weird." They expressed fears of being crazy or perverted. There was always a nagging sense of guilt and shame. Thus, interpersonal learning with peers was aborted early in new relationships. This increasing isolation of the victim, when allowed to continue, probably has the most corroding effect on long-range development because the victim is deprived of all corrective experiences with the peer group.

The data in this study suggest that the experience of incest compounds the problems of sexual development. The sexual relationship with the father contributes to a sense of confusion of love and affection with sex.

Finally, the study indicates that there is a relief of symptoms and changes in behavior once the victim purges herself of the incest secret. It appears that victims who receive acceptance and support from significant others—therapists, friends, other family members, understanding lovers and mates—are better able to remediate the developmental stages they did not successfully complete.

Recommendations

The findings of this study have provided some answers to questions regarding the long-term consequences of a childhood sexual experience with the father. However, much remains to be done. Incest is probably not on the increase, but rather we are seeing the effects of better detection and reporting. Nonetheless, incest needs to be brought into the open, much as rape was ten years ago, for public discussion and recognition. Public information campaigns need to be aimed at demystifying and desexualizing the subject.

I see a need for many educational programs to be developed. First and foremost, programs aimed at prevention, detection, and intervention on behalf of sexually abused children need to be developed and incorporated into school curricula. Television commercials, telephone hotlines, and billboards need to alert children of people and/or telephone numbers to contact for help.

Educational programs need to be developed and presented to lay persons as well as to professionals. The target group would include anyone who has frequent contact with children, such as teachers, parents, school counselors, day-care attendants, social workers, ministers and priests, nurses and physicians, law-enforcement personnel, and mental health professionals. These people are in strategic positions to detect abuse. It is crucial that they become aware of the dynamics in incestuous families, and that they learn how to identify high-risk families. They need to be advised of the reporting laws in their state. Finally, they need to be aware of what services are available in their community and how to obtain them for everyone involved—the victim, the perpetrator, and possibly the entire family.

Clinicians need to become sensitized to sexual-abuse issues so they will be comfortable with clients who present these problems. They must not allow their own emotions, biases, or morals to interfere with effective therapy. The supportive behavior of professionals can be invaluable in minimizing the effects of sexual abuse.

Programs need to be developed to educate attorneys and judges who frequently come into contact with abusive families through the courts.

Communities need to coordinate their efforts for investigation and intervention. A balance between treatment and prosecution should be sought. Efforts need to be exerted to keep these families together, if possible and if desired by all members. Unless the perpetrator is psychotic or a psychopath, the most humane approach may be for the child to stay in the home and treatment provided to each member of the family. The incest must stop! By keeping the focus on maintaining the family and seeking a therapeutic rather than a punitive approach, reporting of the problem is encouraged. If people think that once a report is made, the child will be taken from the family, the perpetrator immediately jailed, and the entire family made to suffer a public scandal, few reports will be forthcoming. By reducing the occurrence of incest, we, as a society, will take a giant step in solving other societal problems including delinquency, runaways, drug and alcohol abuse, and sexual promiscuity. We will also interrupt the generational cycle of sexual abuse.

I strongly urge victims of sexual abuse to seek both individual and group therapy. Group therapy in particular offers a chance for the "secret" to be revealed and the victim to learn that her secret is not so horrible after all. It can be shared without her being abandoned, rejected, or blamed. The group experience helps the victim to build trust, to learn to be nurtured, to be close to others in a nonsexual way, to learn to relate, and to let go of the responsibility for meeting everyone else's needs. In other words, it offers a chance to remediate the developmental stages that were not adequately completed.

I believe that group therapy is the treatment of choice for adolescent and adult victims of incest. Ideally, a male and a female therapist would colead the group.

We now know that the basic issue in incest is not sex, but rather the need for closeness, love, and nurturing. Unfortunately, sex is used to fill other needs. In incestuous families, the parent turns to the child to get basic emotional needs met, rather than vice versa. These parents have no experience in meeting their needs in a healthy way. Universally, perpetrators of sexual abuse are unable to reach out to others in their daily lives to establish closeness and to receive attention and affection.

Parenting classes are invaluable in teaching incest perpetrators how to meet their needs in nonexploitive ways. Since sex is often the only way they know how to express closeness, these classes need to focus on communication skills, self-concept development, how to make friends, how to get close to others in a nonsexual manner, how to express feelings, and how to receive positive reinforcement in their daily lives. An essential part of preventing incestuous behavior is for the parents to learn how to meet their needs and how to handle stress. It has been my professional experience that the majority of parents who become involved in incest never intended to have sex with their children or to cause them psychological harm. Usually there appears to be little premeditation. The behaviors start out innocently and then escalate until they exceed the appropriate limits.

Although it is impossible to know precisely the extent of harm that results from an incestuous experience during childhood, this study points to the need for additional research.

One reason for the lack of conclusive results is that large numbers of victims have not been systematically followed to adulthood in order to identify the long-term consequences.

Research needs to be conducted comparing victims of incest who have participated in marital, individual, and/or group therapy with those victims of incest who have received no therapy.

Longitudinal studies are needed to compare a child's adjustment at varying periods after the sexual experience with an accepted developmental theory, or with peers who have not had a similar incestuous relationship.

Bibliography

Bandura, A. (1969). Social learning theory of identificatory processes. *In* D. Goslen (Ed.), *Handbook of Socialization Theory and Research*. Chicago: Rand-McNally.

Biller, H.B. (1971). *Father, Child and Sex Role*. Lexington, Mass.: Lexington Books.

Blumberg, M.L. (1978). Child sexual abuse—the ultimate in maltreatment syndrome. *New York State Journal of Medicine, 78*, 612–616.

Boekelheide, P.D. (1978). Incest and the family physician. *The Journal of Family Practice, 6*, 200–210.

Bogdan, R.C., and Biklen, S.K. (1982). *Qualitative Research for Education: An Introduction to Theory and Methods*. Boston: Allyn and Bacon.

Burgess, A.W., Groth, A.N., Holmstrom, L.L., and Sgroi, S.M. (1978). *Sexual Assault of Children and Adolescents*. Lexington, Mass.: Lexington Books.

DeMott, B. (1980). The pro-incest lobby. *Psychology Today, 13*, 11.

DeYoung, M. (1982). Innocent seducer or innocently seduced? The role of the child incest victim. *Journal of Clinical Child Psychology, 11*, 56–60.

Denzin, N.K. (1970). *The Research Act in Sociology—A Theoretical Introduction to Sociological Methods*. London: Butterworth.

Erikson, E.H. (1950). *Childhood and Society*. New York: Norton.

Finkelhor, D. (1979). What's wrong with sex between adults and children? Ethics and the problem of sexual abuse. *American Journal of Orthopsychiatry, 49*, 692–697.

Forward, S., and Buck, C. (1978). *Betrayal of Innocence—Incest and Its Devastation*. New York: Penquin Books.

Freud, S. (1938). Totem and taboo. *Basic Writings of Sigmund Freud*. New York: The Modern Library.

Geiser, R.L. (1979). *Hidden Victims*. Boston: Beacon Press.

Giarretto, H. (1982). *Integrated Treatment of Child Sexual Abuse*. Palo Alto: Science and Behavior Books.

Gruber, K.J., Jones, R.J., and Freeman, M.H. (1982). Youth reactions to sexual assault. *Adolescence, 17*, 35–40.

Hamilton, M. (1977). *Father's Influence on Children*. Chicago: Nelson–Hall.

Herman, J. (1981). *Father–Daughter Incest*. Cambridge, Mass.: Harvard University Press.

James, J., and Meyerding, J. (1977). Early sexual experience and prostitution. *American Journal of Psychiatry, 134*, 1381–1385.

Justice, B., and Justice, R. (1979). *The Broken Taboo*. New York: Human Sciences Press.

Kempe, R.S., and Kempe, C.H. (1984). *The Common Secret—Sexual Abuse of Children and Adolescents*. New York: W.H. Freeman.

Kempe, R.S., and Kempe, C.H. (1978). *Child Abuse*. Cambridge, Mass.: Harvard University Press.

Kinsey, A.C., Pomeroy, W.B., Martin, C.E., and Gebhard, P.H. (1953). *Sexual Behavior in the Human Female*. Philadelphia: W.B. Saunders.

Lamb, M. (1975). Fathers: Forgotten contributors to child development. *Human Development, 18*, 245–266.

LeCompte, M.D., and Goetz, J.P. (1984). *Ethnography and Qualitative Design in Educational Research*. New York: Academic Press.

Lester, D. (1975). *Unusual Sexual Behavior—The Standard Deviations*. Springfield, Ill.: Charles C Thomas.

Levinson, D.L. (1978). *The Seasons in a Man's Life*. New York: Ballentine Books.

Masters, W.H., Johnson, V.E., and Kolodny, R.C. (1982). *Human Sexuality*. Boston: Little, Brown.

Meiselman, K.C. (1981). *Incest*. San Francisco: Jossey–Bass.

Patton, M. (1980). *Qualitative Evaluation Methods*. Beverly Hills, Calif.: Sage Publications.

Peters, J.J. (1976). Children who are victims of sexual assault and the psychology of the offender. *American Journal of Psychotherapy, 30*, 398–417.

Ramey, J. (1979). Dealing with the last taboo. *SIECUS, 7*, 1–2.

Rogers, C. (1980). *A Way of Being*. Boston: Houghton Mifflin.

Rosenfeld, A.A. (1977). Sexual misuse and the family. *Victimology: An International Journal, 2*, 226–235.

Schaefer, E. (1965). Children's reports of parental behavior: An inventory. *Child Development, 36*, 413–424.

Sgroi, S.M. (1982). *Handbook of Clinical Intervention In Child Sexual Abuse*. Lexington, Mass.: Lexington Books.

Summit, R., and Kryso, J. (1978). Sexual abuse of children: A clinical spectrum. *American Journal of Orthopsychiatry, 48*, 237–251.

Walters, J., and Stinnet, N. (1971). Parent–child relationships: A decade review of research. *Journal of Marriage and Family Living, 33*, 70–111.

Wells, L. (1981). Family pathology and father–daughter incest: Restricted psychopathy. *Journal of Clinical Psychiatry, 42*, 197–202.

White, K.M., and Speisman, J.C. (1982). *Research Approaches to Personality*. Monterey, Calif.: Brooks/Cole Publishing Co.

White, R.W. (Ed.). (1963). *The study of lives*. New York: Atherton Press.

White, R.W. (1974). *Lives in Progress—A Study of Natural Growth of Personality*. New York: Holt, Rinehart and Winston.

Yates, A. (1982). Children eroticized by incest. *American Journal of Psychiatry, 139*, 482–485.

Index

About the Author

Dianne Cleveland, Ph.D., is currently the director of the Peachtree City Counseling Center in Peachtree City, Georgia. She has had extensive experience working in the field of abuse. While employed by the Georgia Department of Corrections, she worked with incarcerated sexual offenders. In her private practice, she has worked with sexually abused children, adolescents, and adults. She has also worked with entire families where abuse has been discovered and the family desires to try to work through their problems.

Dr. Cleveland earned a B.S. from Auburn University, an M.Ed. from Georgia State University, and an M.Ed. and a Ph.D. from the University of Georgia. She is currently in private practice in Peachtree City, Georgia. She has served as a consultant to many child welfare departments and protective service agencies. She has also been utilized as an expert witness in sexual abuse cases. Dr. Cleveland has conducted training on local, state, national, and international levels on the entire scope of sexual abuse—the perpetrators, the victims, and the dysfunctional families.